D0407733

"Roger Martin and Sally Osberg have written a must-read on how social entrepreneurs are changing the way we 'make the future' to deliver bigger, better results. Their lessons apply to any person or institution seeking to have real impact—whether from the top down or the bottom up. This book could not come at a more important time as the world launches a new agenda for development and inclusive growth."

—**KATHY CALVIN,** President and CEO, United Nations Foundation

"This definitive book, rich with the inspiring stories of successful social entrepreneurs and accompanied by persuasively lucid analysis, points the way for bringing about real change on the ground."

—**JOEL FLEISHMAN,** Professor of Law and Public Policy Studies, Duke University

"*Getting Beyond Better* lays the foundation for a new, rigorous way to conceptualize social entrepreneurship while providing an inspiring, practical guide for changemakers everywhere. A remarkable achievement. Essential reading."

—**MICHAEL GREEN,** CEO, Social Progress Imperative; coauthor, *Philanthrocapitalism*

"In *Getting Beyond Better*, Roger Martin and Sally Osberg remind us why they are the parents of the modern social entrepreneurship movement. Building on their pioneering 2007 *Stanford Social Innovation Review* article, the authors weave the narratives of remarkable people disrupting status quo systems that constrain opportunity for those left out and left behind. This book is a must-read for anyone working to bring about a more just and fair world. Prepare to be motivated and inspired."

—**DARREN WALKER,** President, Ford Foundation

Getting Beyond Better

Getting Beyond Better

How Social Entrepreneurship Works

Roger L. Martin and
Sally R. Osberg

HARVARD BUSINESS REVIEW PRESS
Boston, Massachusetts

Printed in the United States of America

10 9 8 7 6 5 4 3 2 1

Library of Congress Cataloging-in-Publication Data

Martin, Roger L.
Getting beyond better : how social entrepreneurship works / Roger L. Martin and Sally R. Osberg ; foreword by Arianna Huffington.
pages cm
ISBN 978-1-63369-068-4 (hardback)
1. Social entrepreneurship. 2. Social change. I. Osberg, Sally R. II. Title.
HD60.M367 2015
658.4'08—dc23 2015016847

The paper used in this publication meets the requirements of the American National Standard for Permanence of Paper for Publications and Documents in Libraries and Archives Z39.48-1992.

ISBN: 9781633690684
eISBN: 9781633690691

"To try to make the future is highly risky. It is less risky, however, than not to try to make it."

—Peter Drucker

Contents

Foreword

It's always fascinating to talk with people who go beyond dreaming about changing the world, who roll up their sleeves and set about doing it. Roger Martin and Sally Osberg are two of these people—and they know more of these people than most of us do. Through the Skoll Foundation and the Skoll World Forum on Social Entrepreneurship, they have hosted and sparked thousands of conversations with men and women from across the world who have experience and insights about how to move beyond our stale and stuck ways of thinking to bring different perspectives and new solutions to the multitude of crises we are facing.

This experience, together with extensive research into both the public and the private sectors, has led them to a set of principles about social entrepreneurship and its world-changing potential, and they offer those insights here. But this is not a textbook. It's a wonderful collection of stories about inspired and inspiring people who don't accept the prevailing definition of success, who set their sights on creating opportunities not only for material and professional success, but also for lives of well-being, wonder, wisdom, and giving.

It's tempting to think that these are extraordinary individuals who are capable of connecting all the dots in a flash of insight or a killer strategy, people who were born with a talent for solutions and the perseverance to see them through. But in real life, it's not as straightforward as that. Each story involves a journey. Often these social entrepreneurs' journeys begin with the recognition of injustice or suffering, inspiring them to tap into their own inner resources of wisdom to understand the root causes of the misery or injustice, and not only to envision a better way, but to build a model for change and then take that change to scale.

Read the stories closely and you will see how each of these innovators and leaders found renewal and inspiration by working with and staying close to people and communities they loved, people who could recharge their spirits and sense of mission, people who shared their sense of what is possible and helped them make it so.

Molly Melching went to Senegal to study, observed the many ways in which development assistance was missing the mark, and went on to immerse herself in village life until she had built enough knowledge and trust to really begin her work. She developed and expanded a program that engaged women in learning and reflecting on their own human rights—which in turn sparked a growing repudiation of harmful customs and practices, including violence toward women and female genital cutting.

Andrea and Barry Coleman were shocked to discover that transportation was often the missing link in health care in Africa, even in places where governments and charities had invested in transportation needs. They drew on their passion for motorcycles to envision transportation as an integral part of the health system, supplying appropriate vehicles for different urban and rural needs, and the all-important maintenance that kept them reliable.

Adalberto Veríssimo and Carlos Souza Jr. envisioned a time when Brazilian authorities and citizens could control deforestation in the Amazon. They designed a model that monitors the process, making it possible to know, in almost real time, where deforestation occurs.

Paul Farmer and his colleagues created a model for health care in which community health workers accompany patients through all stages of their treatment, helping them address the many issues that affect their well-being. His commitment to making quality health care available to everyone drove him to create not just a model but an academic and professional discipline in the world's leading teaching hospitals, disseminated globally through the Institute for Health and Social Justice.

All of these leaders—disrupters, rebels, changemakers—envision the metrics of the change beyond the usual statistics of wealth, power, graduation rates, decreases in disease, or incarceration. They focus their attention not just on relieving the symptoms of a social problem, but on finding ways to get to the root causes and address them, bringing about positive change on a grand scale in ways others can replicate.

My own experience with change, at the *Huffington Post,* began with the realization that online conversation could become a meeting place, a focus for participation where the ideas of our time would emerge and be shaped. And a lot of people who wanted to be part of that conversation, who society needed to be part of that conversation, were never going to be part of it unless there was a platform to make it easy for them. Remember, this was in 2005, before Facebook, which was born in 2004, had taken off in a big way, and before Twitter, Instagram, and all the other social media platforms that have sprung up since then that have given voice to the voiceless.

We wanted to disrupt the binary way of thinking of the world, and politics as ideological, right and left, because seeing the world in that way causes us to miss out on many opportunities for change and transformation. And we wanted to disrupt the traditional model of journalism—"If it bleeds it leads"—which distorts our worldview by emphasizing calamities and failing to bring us stories of what works. We revered the values of the best of traditional journalism, like fairness and accuracy, speaking truth to power, and deep investigations. But we also wanted to open it up to participation and to invite in those with an eye for solutions alongside those with an eye for disaster.

It was only after the conversation was well under way, with a platform and partnerships to make it possible, and then successful on a global scale, that we saw the real potential of applying a third metric—well-being—to the traditional measures of wealth and power, to define our success as bringing wisdom, well-being, and wonder to the lives of all the communities we serve. I have written about that in *Thrive*, and we have launched multiple sections at the *Huffington Post* to cover all of the new ways in which we are now beginning to approach our lives, values, and priorities.

Getting Beyond Better makes a critical contribution to the integration of that third metric in our view of social innovation and social change. We have become used to the celebration of disrupters in business, in government, in education, in media. What Sally and Roger show is how a select few disrupters—the social entrepreneurs—develop, build, and scale their solutions in ways that bring about truly revolutionary change.

As Roger and Sally point out, one adjustment, one new way of doing things can open possibilities for others, in a cascade of consequences, intended or not. At the *Huffington Post,* we call these "copycat solutions." Gutenberg's press made it possible for ordinary people to read books and have the experience of seeing the world from the point of view of others. The capacity for empathy blossomed, along with the ability to reason and look for the cause of things. And today, massive participation in reporting and commenting on unfolding world events is bringing about a similarly enormous change. We don't yet know where it's leading.

The stories in this book do a tremendous service, not only by exposing us to the work being done by social entrepreneurs who are creatively and relentlessly seeking solutions to existing evils, but by paving the way for even more copycat solutions among those dreaming to change the world.

Arianna Huffington

Introduction

What Is Social Entrepreneurship?

Mother Teresa worked tirelessly to address extreme poverty with the Missionaries of Charity. Martin Luther King Jr. fought for equal rights for all Americans alongside the other founders of the Southern Christian Leadership Conference. Andrew Carnegie spurred the creation of the modern public library. Henry Ford chose to pay his workers enough to be able to buy one of the cars they produced.

Without question, each of these leaders had enormous impact on the world. But were they social entrepreneurs? Calling them by this name, as some might be inclined to do, is based on a desire to validate important work leading to real and significant social benefits. While such an impulse is understandable, it is also unhelpful. If the term *social entrepreneurship* is used to characterize every act of leadership generating public benefit, it will simultaneously become everything and nothing. Striving for social good, as Mother Teresa did, or advocating for social justice, as Martin Luther King did, do not mark one as a social entrepreneur, nor does creating a business that happens to help the world while driving profit, as Henry Ford did. What, then, is social entrepreneurship? For an instructive answer to that question, consider Carnegie.

Carnegie was a steel magnate and one of the wealthiest men of his era. He had been born to a poor Scottish family and immigrated with them to America as a child. As a young man, Carnegie worked as a messenger boy and, as he writes in his 1920 autobiography, "this did not leave much time for self-improvement, nor did the wants of the family leave any money to spend on books."[1] Yet Carnegie yearned to better his mind and saw an opportunity in the generosity of a local businessman.

When Carnegie was a young man in Allegheny, Pennsylvania, Colonel James Anderson, a veteran of the War of 1812 and a pioneer in iron manufacturing, had a personal library of some four hundred volumes to which he regularly allowed his workers access. The young men could take out a book each Saturday, to be returned the following week. Carnegie, who had no such library or any means to access one, wrote a plea to Anderson in the *Pittsburgh Dispatch*. He asked that Anderson open the library not just to his own employees, but to local messenger boys, clerks, and other young workers. Anderson did.

Carnegie recounts: "In this way the windows were opened in the walls of my dungeon through which the light of knowledge streamed in. Every day's toil and even the long hours of night service were lightened by the book which I carried about with me and read in the intervals that could be snatched from duty . . . Books which it would have been impossible for me to obtain elsewhere were, by [Anderson's] wise generosity, placed within my reach."[2]

Late-nineteenth-century America, the world in which Carnegie would prosper, was a place of growth and progress. It was also a place of poverty and discord. While the industrial revolution created previously unimagined economic opportunities, it did not create a level playing field. Inequality, fostered by differences in education and opportunity, remained (and remains) a feature of American society. For instance, a bright young working boy like Andrew Carnegie had no meaningful access to books after the end of his public education. They were simply too expensive for the average family to afford. Rich Americans, by contrast, had ready access to books through their private family libraries. As a result, the rich were continuously able to upgrade their knowledge and put it to use in a way that the poor could not. This created a closed loop of privilege and access—an unhappy but stable status quo.

Carnegie was profoundly grateful to Anderson and considered access to Anderson's library to be a determining factor in his own success. Years later, he decided to extend that light of knowledge beyond the small circle in Allegheny of which he'd been part to cities and towns across America. How? Through the establishment of free public libraries. Carnegie felt that public libraries would help produce the informed citizenry on which democratic society—and, not coincidentally, the free enterprise system that had made him so wealthy—depends. But he didn't just start building libraries anywhere and everywhere. Instead, he created a system that could outlive the people who built it, carefully codifying the terms for his support before providing funds to a community. These terms, which came to be known as the Carnegie Formula, were that prospective recipients must: demonstrate the need for a public library; provide the building site; commit, by raising or allocating taxes, to dedicating an amount equivalent to 10 percent of the cost of the library's construction annually to its operation; and promise free service to all. When a town met the criteria, Carnegie, and later his endowed foundation, the Carnegie Corporation of America, would partner with the community, providing a stream of funds to build its library.

During the thirty-six years in which Carnegie's program operated, it funded the creation of more than twenty-five hundred libraries, almost seventeen hundred in the United States alone (the rest were principally in Britain, Ireland, and Canada). This is remarkable, considering that Carnegie might simply have opened his personal library to members of his community, as Colonel Anderson had done. He could just as easily have stopped after building his first two libraries, one in the town of his birth, Dunfermline, Scotland, and the second in his American hometown of Allegheny, leaving other philanthropists to do the same for their own towns. But he didn't. He did far more, and aimed at a much bigger change. In so doing, he went beyond making his own community, or even a smattering of others, better.

By 1919, Carnegie libraries represented half of all the libraries in the United States.[3] With his innovative approach, he changed the prevailing conditions he'd experienced firsthand as a boy. Through his national network of public libraries, Carnegie transformed a stable but unhappy status quo, in which advanced knowledge was principally accessible to the rich, to a far more optimal state in which knowledge was more equally accessible to all.

What Carnegie achieved might today be called social entrepreneurship. The phenomenon isn't new. But as an idea, an organizing structure and a movement, social entrepreneurship has migrated from the fringes of society to the center only over the last two decades. We have had the great privilege of watching and participating in that shift from our vantage point as directors (plus, in Sally's case, CEO) of the Skoll Foundation. Since the foundation was established in 1999, social entrepreneurship has garnered ever more attention and credibility, even earning two Nobel Peace Prizes: Grameen Bank's Muhammad Yunus in 2006 and GoodWeave's Kailash Satyarthi in 2014.

Yet, for all its success, the nature and boundaries of social entrepreneurship remain in question. Just what is social entrepreneurship, and who can legitimately be considered a social entrepreneur? How do successful social entrepreneurs do what they do, and what can be learned from them? If social entrepreneurship is to continue to grow and become even more central to the transformation of societies and the world, we need clear, useful answers to those questions. We need not just a definition of social entrepreneurship but also a roadmap to guide current and aspiring social entrepreneurs, no matter their sector or job description, toward sustainable change.

Building a Theory

Social entrepreneurs are sometimes seen as doers, rather than thinkers. In our view, they are clearly both, and will be aided by a more robust theory of social entrepreneurship as they continue to advance both thinking and action. The theory and framework put forward in this book have emerged over the past fifteen years. Over that time, we have taken a practitioner's approach. We have worked closely with social entrepreneurs, funding them, advising them, and supporting them during periods of turmoil and transition. The entry point for our work has been the Skoll Awards for Social Entrepreneurship. To date, this awards program has provided recognition and funding to almost one hundred social entrepreneurial organizations and their leaders, all selected for evidence that they are driving positive change throughout the world. The work of these women, men, and organizations, along with their challenges and successes, has served as a kind of developmental lab for clarifying what social entrepreneurship is and how it works. It serves as the basis and motivation for this book.

As fellow travelers with the social entrepreneurs we support, we have come to see ourselves as what the late Donald Schön called *reflective practitioners.* Reflective practitioners think in action; that is, they practice while reflecting mindfully on their actions, in order to continuously improve both their theories and their practices.[4] In an emergent field like social entrepreneurship, reflective practice is particularly important and difficult. It is important because practitioners need to construct their fields through intelligent trial, error, and theory-building. But it is also difficult because emergent fields are amorphous; it is no easy feat to productively reflect on something that is not yet well-defined and rapidly changing.

It is often said that if you want to learn something, teach it. Our variant on this proverbial wisdom? If you want to learn something about how to make a positive contribution to the world, create an awards program for it! In the spring of 2004, as we sifted through the applications for the first Skoll Awards for Social Entrepreneurship, we came to understand at a visceral level that we needed a clearer definition of social entrepreneurship, a richer set of criteria for determining the profile for a social entrepreneur, and a way to distinguish between the qualities and achievements of different social entrepreneurs. Clearly, we had work to do.

In 2007, *Stanford Social Innovation Review* published the initial fruits of our labor, an article titled "Social Entrepreneurship: The Case for Definition."[5] In it, we strove to create a more precise definition of social entrepreneurship by making two important distinctions. The first was between two types of actions: direct versus indirect. A direct action is one an actor takes personally in order to bring about a specific desired outcome. An indirect action is one in which the actor convinces another person or entity to take the specific action that brings about the desired outcome. The second distinction we made was between two types of outcomes: maintenance or incremental improvement of the current system versus transformation of the current system to a new, more optimal system.

These distinctions were critical to our understanding of social entrepreneurship, because they enabled us to distinguish among three groups that have often been conflated: social service providers, social advocates, and social entrepreneurs (see figure I-1).

Social service providers have a long and noble history of working to make communities and the world more equal, safer, healthier and, well, better. These kinds of people and organizations are vital to the well-being of our society. Social service providers, we argued in the article, take *direct action* in a given situation. But they *leave the existing system in place* while seeking to reduce its negative effects. For example, a

FIGURE I-1

Forms of social engagement

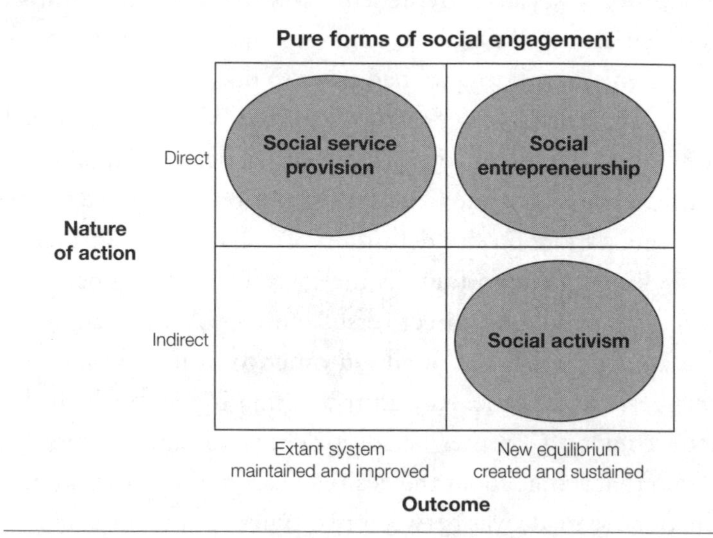

food bank works directly to ameliorate the effects of poverty, providing food to families in desperate need. This food relieves the family's hunger that day, but it doesn't fundamentally change the dynamic that leaves the family so poor that it needs to use the food bank the next week and the next, etc. Similarly, at a global scale, Mother Teresa's Missionaries of Charity works directly to reduce the pain and suffering of the poor and destitute around the world. It is an exemplary social service provider, and the world would be a worse place without it. But it doesn't change the drivers of poverty so much as seek to mitigate its worst effects.

Social advocates too have made our world a far better place. In contrast to social service providers, social advocates work *indirectly*, advocating for legislative changes that can *transform the environment* in question. Martin Luther King Jr. and the Southern Christian Leadership Conference advocated to transform America's treatment of African Americans and other disadvantaged minorities. They fought to end race-based discrimination and implement equal rights legislation in the United States. To produce such sweeping change, though, they needed others to act—in this case, the federal and state governments that could actually pass new legislation enshrining more equal rights. Only with new legislation in place would such fundamental and permanent beneficial change take hold.

Of course, social advocates needn't have the global stature of Dr. King, nor is it always the case that the issues they target are all-encompassing. Social advocates work with all levels of government to create lasting, significant change in a variety of domains, from marriage rights to clean water to local development issues. What makes them social advocates, rather than simply lobbyists, is their desire to transform a suboptimal societal status quo. The lobbyist, in contrast, seeks to bring about a particular benefit—also often through legislation—that accrues to a discrete agent and not to the socially disadvantaged or to society at large. Lobbyists for the tobacco industry may argue that they are protecting the rights of smokers, but in fact they are protecting the economic interests of tobacco companies over the collective best interest of society.

Social entrepreneurs, we argued in the article, can be contrasted with both social service providers and social advocates in that social entrepreneurs both take direct action *and* seek to transform the existing system. They seek to go beyond better, to bring about a transformed, stable new system that is fundamentally different than the world that preceded it. Carnegie aimed at and achieved transformative change rather than a small improvement in the status quo. He wanted free, open access to books for all, rather than a reduction in the costs of books so that a few more people could afford them or access to free books for a small segment of the population. He envisioned a whole new state of affairs in which knowledge was far more accessible than it had been before. He took direct action; he didn't advocate to the government that it should build libraries. He worked with cities and towns, deploying his own money to catalyze their commitment and rolled out his library initiative in accordance with his own criteria.

Building on these two distinctions, social entrepreneurship, we said, can be defined as having the following specific characteristics:

- The identification of a stable but inherently unjust equilibrium that causes the exclusion, marginalization, or suffering of a segment of humanity—a group that lacks the financial means or political clout to effect transformational change on its own.

- The development, testing, refining, and scaling of an equilibrium-shifting solution, deploying a social value proposition that has the potential to challenge the stable state.

- The forging of a new stable equilibrium that unleashes new value for society, releases trapped potential, or alleviates suffering. In this new state, an ecosystem is created around the new equilibrium that sustains and grows it, extending the benefit across society.

Unlike social service providers, social entrepreneurs explicitly aim to permanently and systematically transform a miserable or unfair societal condition. Unlike social advocates, social entrepreneurs act directly, creating a product, service, or methodology that spurs the transformation of the status quo.

Our purpose in making this argument is not to claim that social entrepreneurship is better than social service provision or social advocacy. Many organizations that take indirect action or seek to ameliorate rather than transform do excellent and important work; they merely don't fit under the umbrella of social entrepreneurship.

At the outset, our aim in forging this definition was purely pragmatic. We needed a clear definition that would enable us to identify and select credible—indeed, exemplary—social entrepreneurs for the Skoll awards program. We worried that if we spread the program across too wide an array of organizations, we would fail to build the field of social entrepreneurship effectively. We believed then, and continue to believe, that governments and charitable organizations around the world should fund and support social service providers, social advocates, and social entrepreneurs. But we have focused our efforts on the last of these three, more sharply defining social entrepreneurship and teasing out its distinctive elements as a means to distinguish them from others.

Equilibrium Change

In considering social entrepreneurship, the concept of *equilibrium change* looms large in our thinking. An equilibrium is a balanced, stable system. Left alone, a system in equilibrium will persist in its current state, according to its current structure. The system may well be corrupt, or evil, or unfair, but its forces are in balance and will remain so without intentional action to shift it (and sometimes it will remain even in the face of such action). A system of actors can and often will produce a relatively stable equilibrium that is unpleasant and unproductive for some of those actors, typically for the most underprivileged and marginalized. Carnegie's world, for instance, was in a stable state when it came to access to books; only a transformative shift would afford the majority of people broad access to them. Without such an intervention, things would have continued as they were.

Education systems for the rural poor are another example of a stable but unhappy equilibrium. Across the world, educational inequality represents a long-standing equilibrium. Children from middle-class and, especially, wealthy families have disproportionate access to the best educational opportunities—they attend fine schools where they benefit from the best teachers, curricula, and pedagogy that money can buy. They achieve higher levels of educational attainment, too, further extending their economic advantage. This is true even in the United States: According to the Pew Research Center, "Among millennials ages 25 to 32, median annual earnings for full-time working college-degree holders are $17,500 greater than for those with high school diplomas only. That gap has steadily widened for each successive generation in the latter half of the 20th century."[6]

In the 1970s, Colombia faced the same fundamental equilibrium, even more starkly. At the time, the country was mired in political conflict between the government and left-wing guerillas. The drug trade was growing, driving economic growth but producing violence and uncertainty. The education system was faltering, especially in rural regions where there were simply too few teachers, too poorly trained. As University of California professor E. Mark Hanson observed in his study of the country's education reform, "The 1973 census revealed that the 33.6% of the labor force that had no schooling was concentrated in the rural areas . . . Even though the adult literacy rate increased from 63% in 1960 to 81% in 1975, the rural illiteracy rate was three times that found in urban areas."[7]

The key actors in Colombia's educational system were:

- The government, mandated to provide education to the country's children, but constrained by limited resources and competing imperatives
- Administrators managing school districts, striving to extend dollars as far as possible while recognizing the limitations created by the small scale and relative inaccessibility of rural schools
- Teachers who, despite very minimal training and few supplies, were left alone in their classrooms, often responsible for children across all grades in a single room
- Parents who would choose to either send their children to school with an eye to the future or to keep them at home to work the field or earn a living to support the family in the present
- Students who struggled to learn in suboptimal conditions or who opted out entirely to support their families

The resulting equilibrium was quite stable, held in place by all of the players—each of whom saw the status quo as simply how things ever had been and ever would be. The children of Colombia, and the rural kids in particular, were locked into a miserable system that afforded them little hope of change.

Faced with this structure, the social service provider would accept (grudgingly, of course) the wretched status quo but work hard to ameliorate its negative effects, perhaps by fundraising to provide textbooks or to pay for some additional teachers in rural communities. The social advocate would target the situation by pressuring the Colombian government to change teacher-training regulations or to increase funding to rural schools. The social entrepreneur would attack the system directly, endeavoring to provoke a shift to a new equilibrium, one that would prove both stable and more favorable to the heretofore-disadvantaged children. Which is just what Vicky Colbert did.

Born in Colombia, Colbert had studied sociology and education both at home and abroad. Fresh from a master's program at Stanford University, she returned to Colombia determined to apply all she had learned about how children learn to her country's education system. She took a job in the Ministry of Education as the project coordinator for rural schools and set about changing them from within. At the time, a classroom in Colombia looked much like classrooms around the world—a teacher standing at the front, conducting lessons on a range of subjects from old textbooks. Learning was driven by centralized mandates and imposed timetables, rather than by a child's natural curiosity. It was seen as an individual activity in which peers could do little to contribute to a child's progress (and lots to derail it). Education consisted largely of the memorization and regurgitation of facts.

In her own training and research, Colbert had been exposed to a range of learning models that suggested this was the worst possible approach. So she worked with local teachers and encouraged schools to move to cooperative learning methods and to self-paced instruction, in which children help to architect their own learning. She helped teachers shift from lecturing to facilitating group learning, working with small groups of children at a time to spur their thinking and direct their inquiry. The focus, she argued, should not be on literacy and numeracy for their own sake, but on key life skills as well, including learning to learn, thinking critically, working with others, and making effective decisions. The school itself, Colbert believed, should operate as a self-governed community, in which teachers, parents, and students all have a meaningful say in how things are done. This was the approach to learning in use at the best private schools in the world. Colbert wanted to bring the same approach to the poorest children in Colombia, believing, fundamentally, that all children deserve access to the best education has to offer.

As she worked with teachers and schools, Colbert saw powerful changes in individual classrooms. But she also recognized the limitations of a classroom-by-classroom, school-by-school approach. So, she founded Escuela Nueva (literally, New School), an NGO aimed at codifying and sharing this pedagogical approach for use across Colombia. As she built out her model, she returned again and again to key principles: the curriculum had to be something that could be delivered by the teachers already in the system, it had to be politically feasible and palatable to the strong unions, and it had to be financially sustainable. She was determined to find a holistic solution: "Instead of tackling each of the problems in isolation, it was extremely important to start thinking systemically," she recalls.[8]

Within ten years, the Escuela Nueva model became national policy in Colombia. It has since expanded to Vietnam and Brazil. A 1992 World Bank evaluation of Colombia's schools concluded that poor children educated according to Colbert's principles generally outperformed their better-off peers in traditional schools. A 2000 UNESCO study found that, next to Cuba, Colombia did the best job in Latin America of educating children in rural areas.[9]

For the rural students of Colombia, this new educational platform fundamentally shifted the equilibrium. Under the new, more optimal state, twenty thousand schools adopted an approach that produced better educational outcomes at a cost similar to that incurred by those operating within the old paradigm. This doesn't, of course, mean that the new system is perfect. Escuela Nueva, like many organizations, has its detractors. But few can argue the kids were better off in the old equilibrium than in the new one.

Colbert's work gets to the core of what makes social entrepreneurs distinctive. Social entrepreneurs seek to shift a stable but suboptimal equilibrium in a way that is neither entirely mandated nor entirely market-driven. They create new approaches to old and pernicious problems. And they work directly to tip society to a new and better state. We explore the idea of equilibrium change more fully in chapter 1 and turn to the forces that enable it in chapter 2.

How Social Entrepreneurship Works: A Framework

In the years since we first articulated this definition, working assiduously to support organizations in the business of equilibrium change, we have learned much that goes beyond what we first wrote in the article.

First, true equilibrium change is a high bar. It is exceedingly difficult to produce a meaningful shift to a new stable state. There are many more successful social service providers and social advocates than there are successful social entrepreneurs. In part, this is why we believe so fervently in investing in, connecting, and celebrating social entrepreneurs. We need many more of them, and they need help to achieve their ambitions.

Second, equilibrium change takes time. Existing equilibriums are stable for a reason: the forces at work keep the elements in balance. Just as water will find its own level, social forces will find a resting place, an equilibrium. Moving from one stable state to a new one, therefore, is rarely a smooth and uncontested process. It is not always clear during the transition that the new state will be achieved. In this book, we will discuss several cases of equilibrium change-in-progress. We hope that most will prove successful. We know some won't. Over time, patience and, ultimately, judgment will be required to tell one from the other.

Third, there is a deeper connection between social entrepreneurship and social advocacy than we first conceived. Social advocacy can powerfully enhance and accelerate the pace of equilibrium change. Vicky Colbert, as we've seen, created a transformational student-led approach to schooling rural Colombian children through Escuela Nueva. In this, she was a prototypical social entrepreneur—taking direct action to change an equilibrium. Then, as a social advocate, she pushed the Colombian government to adopt the curriculum more broadly. She advocated so effectively, in fact, that the government appointed her Minister of Education, enabling her to scale her model across the country far more quickly than she could have done school by school.

Beyond these three lessons, we have also seen a distinct pattern in the way that social entrepreneurs do their work. This pattern, which we have structured as a four-stage process, forms the second part of this book. When we look at cases of successful social entrepreneurship—cases in which true equilibrium change was imagined, enacted, and sustained—we can discern a heuristic, a set of actions that seem to guide an enterprise toward success. This model for equilibrium change should not be thought of as a simplistic recipe, but rather, as a framework for thinking about the work of social entrepreneurship as a process. The four stages are illustrated in figure I-2, emanating out from the center in waves.

The stages are:

1. **Understanding the world.** The paradox of social transformation is that one has to truly understand the system as it is before any serious attempt can be made to change it. Yet those who understand the status quo best are often those most deeply invested in the current system, while those who see the imperative for change most clearly tend to sit outside the system, looking in. Effective social entrepreneurs acknowledge

FIGURE I-2

Stages of transformation

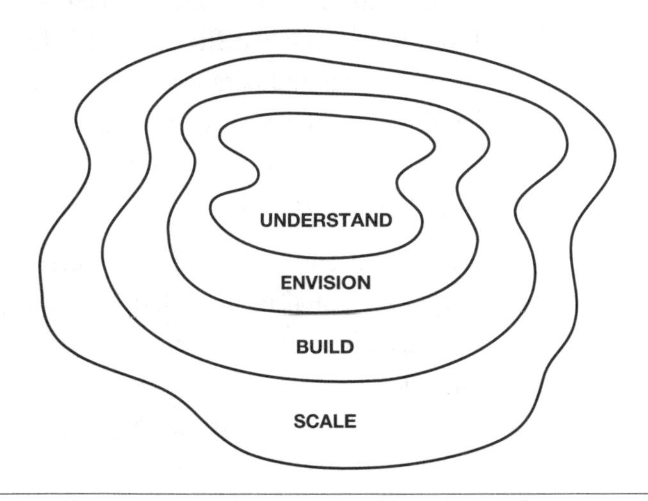

this dynamic and find a way to navigate it, a process we explore in chapter 3.

2. **Envisioning a new future.** To make a positive difference, every change agent, whether a social entrepreneur or not, needs to set a direction. Successful social entrepreneurs set the bar high, envisioning fundamental equilibrium change for specific, targeted constituents. In chapter 4, we discuss how they envision a stable and sustainable world that exists on a new, substantially healthier plane for that targeted population and, often, for society at large.

3. **Building a model for change.** To bring a vision to life, social entrepreneurs must apply creativity and resourcefulness to building a model for change—one

that is sustainable in that it reduces costs or increases value in a systemic and permanent way that can be quantified and captured. In our view, social entrepreneurs don't build innumerably different models for change; there are themes and parallels across success stories. In chapter 5, we articulate a set of specific mechanisms we see employed successfully across contexts to transform equilibriums.

4. **Scaling the solution.** Scalability is a critical feature of successful social entrepreneurship. Models that require constant reapplication of the same level of investment regardless of scale will commonly fail to produce sustainable equilibrium change. Such an approach may be too expensive to achieve transformational scale, especially when intended beneficiaries are unable to pay for the benefit. In chapter 6, we explore ways effective social entrepreneurs scale their impact.

Under Construction: Building Social Entrepreneurship

We want to be clear: we are in the middle of a journey, not at the end of one. We believe we have learned much that can be useful, even as we freely admit much remains to be learned.

In writing this book—indeed, in building our theory of social entrepreneurship—we are deeply mindful of those who have come before us and the debt we owe to them. We and many others in the field, especially in the United States, look to John W. Gardner as a seminal figure. Gardner served as

President Lyndon Johnson's Secretary of Health, Education, and Welfare and was one of the architects of the Great Society. As president of the Carnegie Corporation of New York, he carried on Andrew Carnegie's legacy in myriad ways, perhaps none as powerfully as in supporting the Corporation for Public Broadcasting, which led to two new institutions for public learning and discourse: National Public Radio and the Public Broadcasting Service. He was also the founder of multiple organizations including Independent Sector, which brings US nonprofit organizations and foundations together, and Common Cause, which works to safeguard the tenets of American democracy. While he never wrote about social entrepreneurship per se, his life's work and his prescriptions for productive citizenship—as described in his 1963 book *Self-Renewal: The Individual and the Innovative Society*—inspired a generation of thinkers and practitioners who would go on to shape the field of social entrepreneurship in line with those ideals.

On the other side of the Atlantic was Lord Michael Young, a sociologist of prodigious accomplishments, among them the creation of the Open University, which pioneered the concept of distance learning and offered a radically new alternative to the traditional brick-and-mortar model of higher education. Later in life, Young turned more explicitly to the concept of social entrepreneurship, founding the School for Social Entrepreneurs in 1997, an institution that has trained an entire generation of aspiring social entrepreneurs.

Then there is Bill Drayton, whom many of us view as the godfather of modern social entrepreneurship. Drayton wasn't the first to use the term of art, but when he founded Ashoka in 1981 to recognize and support social entrepreneurs, he took a diffuse and emergent phenomenon and gave it a center of gravity. Over the past thirty years, Drayton's organization has identified and elected as "Ashoka Fellows" more than three thousand social entrepreneurs in over seventy countries.[10] As chairman and CEO, Drayton has worked tirelessly, organizing, writing, mentoring, and inspiring others to build the field.

Finally, no list of social entrepreneurship pioneers can be complete without inclusion of Jeff Skoll, the founding president of eBay and, subsequently, founder of both Participant Media and the Skoll Foundation. It is through Skoll, and his invitations to join him at the foundation, that each of us first came to the world of social entrepreneurship. Skoll is clear that his motivation rests squarely on "betting on good people" to drive change where it matters most in the world. It's because of his vision and support that the foundation has become the leading funder of social entrepreneurship in the world and has established the Skoll Centre at the Saïd School of Business at Oxford University, the annual Skoll World Forum (SWF), and the Skoll Awards for Social Entrepreneurship, all levers to advance understanding and practice of social entrepreneurship at work in the world.

Gardner, Young, Drayton, and Skoll came to the field as we did, as practitioners who sought to build and test their theories through action. Of course, a number of others have viewed the field through an academic lens. There is much to be learned by consulting the growing body of academic work on social entrepreneurship, beginning with the groundbreaking work of the late Greg Dees. For those readers who want to delve into this literature, we have included a bibliography listing many of this still-emergent field's key texts and articles. But this book is not meant to be an academic text.

While academic inquiry is an important endeavor—indeed, every field needs the rigor of academic scholarship to pose key questions and establish boundaries—it has not, on the whole, shaped our experience. *Getting Beyond Better* is a book by reflective practitioners. Practicing, soliciting feedback, reflecting on our experience, adjusting, and practicing some more: that is how our theory and framework have evolved.

And so our hope is that this book will be of most use to practitioners. In fact, *Getting Beyond Better* is aimed primarily at four audiences:

First are current and aspiring social entrepreneurs, including students of social entrepreneurship. We hope that the first part of the book helps you to see your (current or prospective) position in the world in ways that will help you productively orient your practice. To that end, we offer insights on processes and models in the second part of the book in order to help you understand your own trajectory and consider whether to refine your current approach or develop a new one.

Second are funders or potential funders of social entrepreneurship, whether individuals or institutions akin in spirit to the Skoll Foundation. In many ways, we built the theories in this book to help us to do our work, and do it more responsibly, at the foundation. We think that many other foundations and individual givers are similarly interested in the promise of social entrepreneurship to transform systems, but admit to feeling challenged in understanding the field. We believe what we share here can help you to identify and assess organizations aiming at change in order to make more effective investments. The more successful investments funders make, the bigger and more successful social entrepreneurship will be—and the greater likelihood that our world will reap the returns.

Third are context regulators of social entrepreneurship. Every organization in society is both constricted and enabled by its legal and regulatory context. Social entrepreneurship is no exception. As a hybrid form of organization that lies somewhere between for-profit business and government agency, social entrepreneurship can be a confusing beast. Some jurisdictions—such as the United Kingdom—have handled the ambiguity better than others. We therefore hope the book can be used as a guide for policymakers and others in a position to consider enabling legislation.

Fourth are teachers of social entrepreneurship. No one knows better than we do how rapidly demand for courses, instruction, and mentorship has grown in recent years. Happily, teaching resources are being created to respond to this need, but we see ample room for more. Our hope is that a book that is clearly anchored in practice will provide one more option for educators to use in teaching social entrepreneurship, supplementing the important work already done by academics and other contributors.

On to Social Transformation

With that, we welcome you enthusiastically to chapter 1, which takes you back in time to fifteenth-century Europe to explore the nature of social transformation. We then move on to the dynamics of social transformation, highlighting the principles and forces that drive it. With this background—much of it familiar but newly framed—under your belt, you will be well positioned to delve into the ways social entrepreneurs produce their transformative changes. We hope you enjoy the journey as much as we have.

Part I

Transformation for Good

Chapter 1

Shifting an Equilibrium

Johannes Gensfleisch zur Laden zum Gutenberg was born at the end of the fourteenth century, just as change was rippling across Europe. The continent was emerging from a century of death and decay in which famine and plague had combined to kill or displace more than a third of its population. It had been a time of social unrest and seemingly unending war. But now, the population was stabilizing, prosperity was returning, and political power was shifting. As the new century progressed, trade flourished, guilds expanded, and the age of exploration began. The Ottoman Empire rose in the East and the Holy Roman Empire's grip on Europe weakened. But these changes would pale in comparison with the shift Gutenberg himself would unleash.

Gutenberg's early career didn't suggest a change agent in the making. The son of a wealthy merchant, he stumbled badly in his earliest ventures—most notably a scheme to make souvenir mirrors for an exhibition of Charlemagne's relics. The highly polished mirrors were to be hawked to pilgrims, who would use them to capture the "holy radiance" emanating from the relics.

The whole enterprise flopped when a flood delayed the exhibition and the hordes of gullible customers failed to materialize. Broke and dogged by unhappy business partners, Gutenberg promised to satisfy his investors not with funds, but with a tantalizing "secret." This turned out to be a new invention: an effective process for printing using movable type.

Like most inventions, Gutenberg's printing press wasn't an entirely new idea; movable type had been invented in China centuries before and had slowly spread across Asia and into Europe. But Gutenberg adapted those existing technologies to make his printing process far faster and more reliable, enabling the production of meaningful quantities of high-quality typeset pages for the first time. His invention encompassed not only his press and its moveable type, but also a casting process that would reproduce his carefully designed dyes, a means to align and space them, and even a special ink that would facilitate printing in color.

Gutenberg's printing press had the potential to shift the production of print from artisans to machines, lowering costs and increasing production. In this way, it was not unlike many other inventions. And like those, the printing press might have remained a promising new technology were it not for what happened next. Gutenberg and others began producing and selling printed materials widely. These publishing businesses would make the written word far more accessible than ever before. By enabling broad access to the printed word, Gutenberg's venture set the stage for widespread literacy and for nothing less than the democratization of knowledge.

Before Gutenberg came along, knowledge in the West was effectively cartelized. The primary form of the written word was the bound book—newspapers, magazines, and other written materials as we know them today didn't exist. Books, which represented the world's collected knowledge, were phenomenally costly to produce, especially since these manuscripts were unique works of art. They were created mainly by priests and monks who dedicated painstaking hours of labor to the calligraphy and illustrations on each page, and who had access to the gold, lapis lazuli, and other precious pigments used for that purpose. As a result, only the church and the wealthiest private citizens could afford to commission and own books. Only they could access knowledge in written form.

For the rest of the world, information was communicated orally and by example. Commoners had little chance to learn to read, not because of a lack of intellect or interest, but because there was no reading material available to them. While the seasonal activities of planting and harvesting were richly captured in illuminations in the *Très Riches Heures du Jean, Duc de Berry*, the working peasants depicted in those pages would not have seen the book or been aware their labors had been recorded. Instead, workers learned how to cultivate the land from their parents, working alongside them in the fields; in turn, they passed on what they had learned, instructing their children through example and narrative. In parish churches and grand cathedrals, religious instruction was communicated (in Latin) from the pulpit. Ordinary folk didn't have access to printed Bibles; they absorbed their religious understanding largely from ritual practice and from interactions with parish priests.

The expensive process of book production ensured not only that knowledge, but the power that comes from possessing it, remained out of reach of the masses. A small minority—the church, landed gentry, and the guilds, all of whom prospered and benefited from the status quo—was able to maintain and enforce an advantage over the majority. Those on the wrong side of the equation had only two choices: settle meekly for their lot in life or struggle in vain against an entrenched system.

Then, with the advent of Gutenberg's press, it became possible to produce the written word at scale. The speed and reliability of the press reduced printing costs enough that many more citizens could afford printed materials. From that point, change came swiftly. Gutenberg's shop in Mainz, Germany, spurred a new industry; by the end of the fifteenth century, printing enterprises were recorded in some 270 cities across Europe. The Age of Enlightenment and the Protestant Reformation subsequently took hold, both enabled by ready access to the written and printed word.

In many ways, Gutenberg was a prototypical entrepreneur. He sought to make his fortune in the world through a commercial enterprise. He looked for an opportunity—an unmet need—and imagined a better answer. He designed a way to meet that need reliably and created a business to exploit that answer. He didn't just invent the printing press; he established a publishing enterprise, aiming (though largely failing) to enrich himself from his invention.

Yet Gutenberg's impact was far bigger than he could originally imagine. He fundamentally reset the way the world works. His invention was world-changing because it addressed not just an individual need but also a much broader social equilibrium. Though it is unlikely he would have framed it this way, Gutenberg moved the world forward because he created a mechanism to successfully shift an unhappy equilibrium to one far beyond better.

Recall that a system is in equilibrium when it is balanced and stable. Such systems tend to be pervasive, self-reinforcing, and persistent. That is not to say they are reasonable, just, or fair. As a steady state, systems in equilibrium are all but invisible to their participants. They can feel natural, even inevitable, as the way things are and ever shall be.

Think of the state of knowledge before the advent of the printing press. Only a small minority held and maintained control over information. Though the precise makeup of these elites shifted over time, the central dynamic—cartelization of knowledge and subjugation of the masses on that basis—did not. With the printing press, Gutenberg altered this stable state. He enabled wider access to information, creating the conditions for mass literacy and a much faster, more profound advancement of knowledge. The first newspaper appeared within sixty years of Gutenberg's invention, as did Shakespeare's first quartos.

Access to the printed word paved the way for a revolution in human thought, as the theses of Martin Luther and works of Enlightenment philosophers like Locke, Hume, and Voltaire could be read and disseminated far more easily than would have been the case in the past. The publishers who followed Gutenberg extended his impact, helping establish and reinforce the new state of the world.

A new and superior equilibrium emerged—not all at once, but in fits and starts, because pervasive change is often bitterly contested—until an equally stable but superior state was produced. In time, the world was positively transformed.

The new equilibrium, it should be noted, isn't perfect. As you'll recall from the story of Andrew Carnegie in the introduction, the printing press didn't provide equal and untrammeled access to books. But it shifted the world from a state in which a tiny few had access to the written word to one in which printed material was widely available to the masses—spurring enormous increases in literacy as access to broadsheets, newspapers, and some books, particularly in an emergent public education system, opened up more broadly. But widespread as such access was, it was not truly comprehensive. Hundreds of years after the advent of the printing press, books still were far more accessible to the rich than to the poor. Hence, Carnegie's own transformation, in a time-honored tradition, was erected on the shoulders of the giants who preceded him.

The Nature of Social Transformation

Social transformation—by which we mean positive, fundamental, and lasting change to the prevailing conditions under which most members of a society live and work—is almost always the result of a successful challenge to an existing equilibrium. Individuals and groups take aim at the status quo, attempting to shift it to a new and superior state in which the prevailing conditions are substantially and sustainably improved for the majority. The path to such transformative change, even when conditions appear ripe, is far from inevitable; nor does it always run smoothly.

To understand just how this kind of social transformation happens, it is helpful to step back and look at transformation in a very different realm: the world of science. The standard narrative of scientific progress goes something like this: scientific understanding moves forward in a steady, if occasionally plodding way, with each scientist building on the work that came before, adding and enriching our shared understanding over time.

In 1962, Thomas Kuhn upended this narrative with his book *The Structure of Scientific Revolutions*.[1] Kuhn argued that scientific knowledge advances not in a steady march from one great thinker to the next but through disruption. Great thinkers, he said, play a role—but not the one we expect. They don't build on the work that preceded them so much as question and redefine it. He explained this theory by contrasting two distinctly different modes of progress: normal science and scientific revolution.

Normal science looks a lot like our traditional slow-and-steady narrative. In normal science, a scientific community operates under a prevailing paradigm—an essential understanding of the world as it relates to a particular area of inquiry. The job of the scientist is to extend and strengthen the central paradigm by pursuing and solving particular puzzles within it. Scientists accept the underlying assumptions of the theory and make progress within it on that basis. This standard progression can be powerfully efficient, enabling deeper understanding over time. But this mode of progress has significant limitations as well. The paradigm demands adherence. Those who question it, or choose to operate outside of it, are seen as wrong-headed; they can be ridiculed, ostracized, and even punished. Why? Because they represent an unwelcome challenge to the status quo, and as such, they must be ignored, suppressed, or quashed. The existing paradigm, as a result, becomes entrenched and ever more dominant—even if it is flawed.

According to Kuhn, the depth of inquiry into the existing paradigm will eventually start to raise challenges to the paradigm itself—data emerges that can seem anomalous or difficult to explain in the context of the existing framework. As these anomalies pile up, they weaken the current paradigm's hold, eventually precipitating a crisis. Sometimes, the crisis can be resolved through further inquiry into the paradigm (through more normal science, in other words). But often, the crisis causes the paradigm itself to be called into question.

Some scientists begin to question fundamental assumptions of the field in crisis, positing new and different paradigms that would explain the anomalies and shift the framework substantially. Kuhn called this stage *revolutionary science*. He described it as a fundamental shift in which the field pivots to a new understanding and new approach. Textbooks are rewritten. Standard procedures are redesigned. Reputations are altered. Outcasts become revered central figures. Then, as the new paradigm becomes established, the community adapts and returns to a normal science approach within the new context. Until the next revolution.

Consider an example familiar to every schoolchild: the Copernican revolution. For centuries, the prevailing view of the scientific community was that the earth was the center of the universe, a stationary point around which the sun, planets, and cosmos moved. Normal science, built on the core theories Ptolemy articulated in the second century, modeled the tracks of celestial bodies around an unmoving earth. By the mid-sixteenth century, though, our ability to track the movements of the stars had advanced to such an extent that cracks were showing in Ptolemy's model. Planets and stars seemed to move in ways that didn't fit the paradigm.

In 1543, astronomer and mathematician Nicolaus Copernicus published *De Revolutionibus Orbium Coelestium* (*On the Revolutions of the Celestial Spheres*), in which he proposed a new cosmology, with the sun at the center and the earth as just one of the planets revolving around it. Copernicus was largely dismissed, in part because his math didn't quite work out. He had the right insight, but the wrong data. He attempted to use the tools of normal science, the models inherited from the ancient Greeks, to map out the movements of the planets around the sun. Try as he might, however, he failed to increase the accuracy of predictions using his new paradigm.

It wasn't until Italian physicist Galileo Galilei articulated a new theory of objects in motion some half a century later that the revolution really took hold. He compensated for the gaps in Copernicus' ideas by hypothesizing that a previously unknown outside force must cause planetary bodies to move in curved paths rather than in straight lines. For his insights, he was condemned as a heretic. Yet a contemporary, Johannes Kepler, and a successor, Isaac Newton, both built on Galileo's work. Ultimately, they established a new paradigm for understanding the universe and affirmed new laws of planetary motion. The revolution was concluded. Normal science was reestablished. Scientists set to work exploring questions within the new paradigm, which would hold for the next three centuries.

This pattern, Kuhn argues, repeats itself across every domain of scientific inquiry. Normal science—acceptance and inquiry into the accepted paradigm—is disrupted and transformed by a period of revolution—radical and seismic changes to scientific understanding. Science progresses, he said, not in steady steps from one great thinker to the next, but in cataclysmic leaps. Kuhn's book, improbably, became one of the most influential books of the twentieth century, altering our understanding of the history and progression of science.

What can we learn from this new understanding of scientific progress to inform our understanding of transformation more broadly? To what extent does Kuhn's model apply beyond the world of science? As we see it, Kuhn's thinking applies in helpful ways. Does the history of art, the social sciences—virtually every area of human inquiry and pursuit—not offer a similar pattern of orthodoxy, challenge, revolution, and reset? Monet and Picasso, Maria Montessori and John Dewey are not so different from Copernicus and Galileo. Beyond explaining scientific progress, Kuhn captures something essential about the way in which our world leaps forward across many different domains of human endeavor. He has captured a pattern that also applies to societies and their changes over time.

As with science, most of the time societies move forward in modest increments as we hone and refine an existing model, accepting the current paradigm and attempting to make headway within it. We accept economic inequality as largely inevitable, for instance, and focus on reducing its negative effects through social programs like food stamps, school lunch programs, and foreign aid. We accept that inefficient markets are just a feature of the world, and create businesses to exploit those inefficiencies rather than creating organizations that eliminate them. Our approach to change in this stage is akin to that exercised in the realm of normal science—we accept the current equilibrium, which remains widely stable, if unhappy. As we have noted, this not to say the progress made within the normal science phase is necessarily unhelpful. Often, individuals and organizations can reduce the worst effects of the current state and make life a little better for those who are most disadvantaged by it.

Actors in the normal phase accept the status quo, the existing paradigm, as largely natural and normal. Governments tweak and adapt legislation with the intention of making things a little better and reinforcing the equilibrium should it falter. In the wake of crises threatening the US economy, for example, legislation such as Sarbanes-Oxley and Dodd-Frank was introduced to prevent business behaviors of the kind that had so disrupted financial markets. Similarly, entrepreneurs find ways to benefit from the status quo, as when traders build complex quantitative models to exploit tiny arbitrage opportunities in inefficient capital markets. Charities, religious organizations, and social service organizations strive to ameliorate the negative effects of the existing equilibrium, applying balms to sore spots, improving access to health care through free and low-cost services, providing food banks and other services to those who cannot afford life's basics, and so on. Life continues on, a little better than it was before. But wholesale transformation—remaking the financial markets, building new ways to create rather than trade wealth, restructuring the social order to redistribute advantages—is largely off the table. Instead, social institutions will try simply to make the best of a bad situation.

But every once in a while, backed by revolutionary rather than normal thinking, a society leaps forward to a fundamentally new equilibrium. The old status quo is left behind, even if it had held stably for centuries, and even if many powerful people and organizations were deeply invested in it. This revolutionary form of agency finds powerful new ways

FIGURE 1-1

Equilibrium change

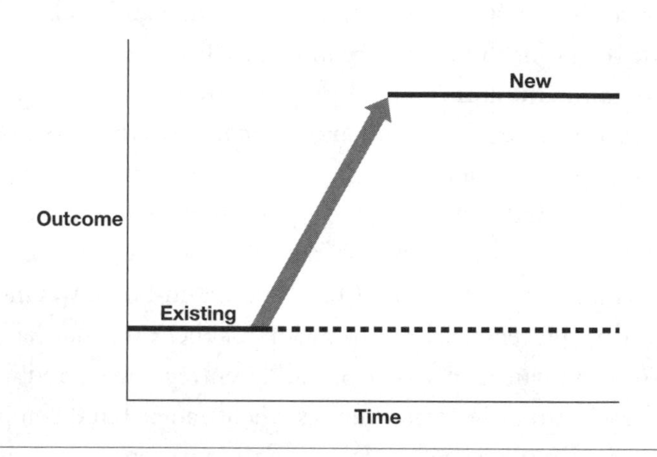

to structure systems, altering fundamentally how they work and the impact they have on us. New forms of government or new enterprises with profoundly different value propositions and dramatically different operating assumptions emerge. A new state of affairs that changes, rather than ameliorates, existing conditions comes to prevail. The fundamental shift can be visualized as a step change, as illustrated in figure 1-1.

Of course, not all revolutionary transformation is successful, nor is it always a step forward. Some avenues of scientific inquiry lead to dead ends; some produce more harm than good—and the same is true in the social realm. Societies falter and fall back. Some shifts prove unsustainable, and the world regresses to its former way of being, at least for a time. In times of war and economic upheaval, for instance, centuries of gain can be demolished in a moment. But some changes endure, scale, and establish a substantially more beneficial equilibrium over the long term.

Most of the work of a society fits into the normal science model. We make the world a little better within the context of an existing paradigm. This is true across many different actors in our society: government, social service providers, even business. Just as governments and social service providers tend to accept the current status quo and work within it, so too do many business leaders. They accept a shared understanding of how markets work, what customers need, and what is possible for an enterprise. They then operate and innovate within that frame, making small changes over time. But not all businesses accept the prevailing paradigm. Some, often entrepreneurs like Gutenberg, question the fundamental prevailing assumptions and attempt to change the game entirely. They seek a revolution. But in their case, they seek a revolution that has the potential to make them rich!

Revolution can come from many quarters, but in our view, it is helpful to frame our understanding of social transformation by looking at two forces that produce transformation in distinctive ways: government and business. Government generates transformative change through policy innovation and by enacting new legal frameworks, while business does so through ventures that create new markets and change the terms of existing ones. In both cases, individuals and institutions tackle an unhappy equilibrium in order to effect large-scale, sustainable change.

Government-Led Transformation

Government, the institutionalized system by which a state is organized and overseen, takes many forms. Over the long reach of history, government bodies tended to be regal (e.g., king, emperor), religious (e.g., the Pope), or tribal (e.g., a chief) in nature. Only relatively recently have we seen the widespread emergence of democratically elected governing bodies. But whether a body claims its right to govern through inheritance or by election, its legitimacy depends on a social contract with its citizens. In return for its right to govern, it must oversee, protect, and manage the state and its citizens. This imperative is strongest in a democracy, but even in a dictatorship, the leader must pay some heed to the needs of citizens or risk deposal. This contract requires dialogue between the state and its citizens. Not surprisingly, much government-led transformation tracks directly from this dialogue; government is pushed by individual citizens to make revolutionary changes and, often, by organized social activists advocating for fundamental change on behalf of their fellow citizens.

A seminal example of this kind of government-led paradigm shift is the Magna Carta, the document signed in 1215 by England's King John in response to intense pressure from wealthy landowners. This "Great Charter" is said to have ushered in the secular rule of law. Before this compact, even the most powerful barons chafed under the status quo, which accorded all power to the reigning monarch. Like a mob boss, the king could make anyone disappear—a power King John himself had used repeatedly to keep his ranks in line. In addition, because the king could seize any property he wished, the incentive for investment was diminished and the economy hamstrung. Why invest in building anything that might attract the king's attention and be snatched away? The state was in an unhappy equilibrium in which the king possessed all the power and was quick to exercise it in ways that prevented economic growth and stalled advancement of social well-being.

Strikingly, King John's disgruntled barons, bishops, and abbots eschewed the well-established practice of overthrowing the current king and attempting to install one more sympathetic to their interests. That kind of rebellion would have signaled an acceptance of the fundamental structure of the existing equilibrium. It would have constituted an attempt to ameliorate it, but ultimately would have reinforced the all-encompassing authority of a reigning monarch. The figure at the top would change, but the structure supporting him would not. And who could know what might happen with the next new king, and the next, and the next? Instead, at considerable risk to their lives, England's upper echelons charted another path—one that would attempt to shift the equilibrium permanently by securing their rights.

Over time, the principles put forth in the Magna Carta secured a profound transformation to the way English society worked. As a new mandate enshrined as law, the Magna Carta forced the king to relinquish his unlimited powers, distributed new rights to ranking members of England's feudal society, and thereby laid the foundation for the distribution of far-reaching benefits to citizens in centuries to come.

A more current example of government-led transformation is the US Civil Rights Act of 1964. The United States was famously founded on the notion of equality and opportunity for all. It was also founded on the backs of African slaves, who were deemed to be property and therefore undeserving of basic rights. Even after a punishing civil war and the mandated abolition of slavery across the country, a deeply unjust equilibrium prevailed for another century. Government legislation and social norms conspired to keep African Americans (and other visible minorities) poor, badly educated, and economically disadvantaged, which effectively trapped most in a permanent underclass. Equality and opportunity remained out of reach, especially in the segregated South.

Civil rights activists, including Martin Luther King Jr. and Malcolm X, advocated long and hard for change, eventually producing a groundswell the government couldn't ignore. The result was the Civil Rights Act, which brought about a step-function change to the unjust equilibrium by outlawing racial, ethnic, religious, and gender discrimination, including the racial segregation of public schools. It also put a legal end to the discriminatory application of voter registration requirements, giving African Americans full rights to the electoral process for the first time. Still, the work required to ensure the universal application of civil rights in America may never be truly finished (as witnessed by recent battles over same-sex marriage, criminal justice, voter ID requirements, and immigration rights), but a leap of progress was clearly made and a new equilibrium achieved.

Of course, government-led transformation needn't happen only at federal levels. Local governments can, and do, transform their communities through policies like mandated recycling and infrastructure investments that change how people live, travel, and interact.

Regardless of the particular geographic scope, in government-led transformation, the effects of the change are wide reaching, with benefits (and costs) accruing across a society. Business-led transformation, on the other hand, can transform and improve our lives, but only as long as customers can pay for the innovation.

Business-Led Transformation

A business is fundamentally an organization engaged in the trade of goods, services, or both, to customers, typically in exchange for money. In historical terms, business innovation did not emerge as an important social phenomenon until relatively recently; the role of business entities as catalysts of social transformation didn't really flourish until the Industrial Revolution, when businesses began to grow far bigger than previously possible. With profound scale, a positive cycle developed in which one innovation (for example, the steam engine) could enable and spur the creation of a transformational industry (the railway) that could change how communities and societies worked.

While economic output is only one measure of a society's advancement, it is not an unimportant one. In real terms, the world's economic output had been increasing at the anemic rate of 0.22 percent per year for the thousand years leading up to 1820, the middle of the first Industrial Revolution. In the next 180 years, growth increased tenfold and the world advanced at a 2.2 percent compound annual rate. That means that in the last 180 years, the world's output increased fifty times while in the previous thousand years, it had only increased sevenfold. The dramatic increase over the last 180 years was largely the result of the emergence of business innovation as a positive transformational force.

How does the world move forward through business-led transformation? Again, we turn to a familiar example: Thomas Edison and the electric lightbulb. Until 150 years ago, we lived by candlelight. A good alternative to sitting in the dark, the candle was inherently dangerous thanks to the open flame involved, messy due to the smoke produced, unreliable as it was subject to extinction by a breeze, and relatively ineffective in actually generating light, its whole purpose in the first place. The incrementally better oil lamp offered a more protected flame, reduced the risk of fire and inadvertent extinguishment, produced less smoke, and was engineered to produce a greater amount of light. It could also burn for a longer time, due to a design that gave its wick access to a built-in reservoir of oil. However, it was still basically a better candle, the best option available when the sun went down.

In 1879, Thomas Edison invented the first commercial electric incandescent lightbulb. Note that he didn't invent the electric light—Humphry Davy did that in 1800, but Davy's invention didn't lend itself to commercial production. Nor did any of the electric light creations in the ensuing seventy-nine years, demonstrating that technological invention by itself is not a transformer of equilibriums.

Edison's lightbulb was only part of his innovation. Like Gutenberg before him, he sought to leverage the impact of his invention with a business venture, creating the essential infrastructure to manufacture and market his device. He built an electric company. As his new business took hold and then took off, Edison dramatically improved a suboptimal and dimly lit equilibrium by establishing and selling safe, clean, and effective light. Economically, his invention and its supporting enterprise were utterly transformative, allowing factories to operate their expensive equipment around the clock on multiple shifts, which dramatically accelerated industrial productivity. At home, electric light created a new cadence to the day, extending the evening as long as one might wish.

Edison's enterprise attacked an unpleasant equilibrium for customers who could pay. The resulting revenue produced profits that enabled Edison's enterprise to grow and thrive—in fact, it would go on to become one of the world's largest and most successful businesses, General Electric Corporation. Today, GE consistently ranks among the twenty most valuable companies in the world by market capitalization. Edison's innovation and company shifted an unhappy equilibrium—a sooty, dark, candlelit world—into a better one, from which the industrialized world continues to benefit dramatically.

A more recent example of this kind of transformative, business-led social innovation emanated from Cupertino, California, courtesy of Steve Jobs and Steve Wozniak. Before they arrived on the scene, though, a first transformative change had already taken place. Developed through the first half of the twentieth century and becoming more widely available in the second, computers represented an equilibrium-shifting advance from the abacus and from paper and pen. But in their original form, computers soon came to represent a less-than-happy equilibrium of their own. By design, mainframe computers, which were massive, expensive, and housed centrally, held all the software, computational power, and data for their organizations. Corporate users had input terminals, through which they could access the mainframe, but with little control, ability to customize, or flexibility. All the real power of the computer rested with the mainframe, and with the information technology staff who treated it as their own, precious protectorate. Of course, computer technology even at this stage offered significant benefits over a world with no computers. But it wasn't particularly pleasant or productive.

A personal computer, which possessed its own processing power and housed its own data, could free its user from the shackles of the mainframe and from the bureaucratic information technology departments who tended them. This was the contribution of Jobs and Wozniak. A couple of computer-obsessed autodidacts, together they created the world's first commercial personal computer, the Apple II, in 1977. As with Edison's lightbulb, their invention wasn't the first device of its kind. The first personal computer was the 1974 Altair computer kit. Apple II wasn't even Apple's first personal computer. But it was the first personal computer that was widely available commercially, with a real supporting enterprise behind it.

The Apple II heralded a new era and a new, more productive equilibrium of user-controlled computing. In relatively short order, an entire ecosystem of hardware, software, and peripheral suppliers built up to serve users' every whim in this new equilibrium. Today, it is hard to imagine not having massive computer power at your own disposal (in fact, in your pocket—thanks, again, to Apple).

Jobs and Wozniak made the world better for their customers, but the goal of their enterprise was not just social change and benefit to society. It was also (arguably largely) to create a viable, profitable business for themselves. They sought to change the world (or as Jobs so memorably put it, to "make a little dent in the universe") and to earn a living in the process.[2] They tackled an unhappy equilibrium through a commercial path, hoping to make money for themselves. Like Edison, they moved the world forward—differently than did King John and his barons or Lyndon Johnson and civil rights advocates—but equally significantly.

As with government-led innovation, business-led innovation is not purely the domain of massive and powerful organizations. Edison, Jobs, and Wozniak set out to transform equilibriums before their enterprises achieved substantial size. Any organization that sees a suboptimal equilibrium and sets out to change it via a commercial path is engaged in business-led transformation, regardless of the size of the organization or market.

Another Way

Government-led and business-led transformations mark two paths toward equilibrium change. Through their distinctive institutional forms, governments and businesses can move the world forward. They can act, in effect, as agents of social revolution. In both modalities, orthodoxy is challenged, a new way of thinking is introduced, and a different model is established. Thereafter, normal society, like normal science, prevails. This normal period may last for a short or long time, but it represents a stable way of being that is only truly disrupted when the next revolutionary successfully alters the status quo.

Such transformation is relatively rare across the span of history. It is inherently challenging to pull off, and often takes a prod from the outside—committed social activists or emerging competitive threats—to get going. This makes sense; after all, government and business are typically deeply invested in the status quo of the normal phase. Unsurprisingly, they are usually reluctant to disrupt themselves. This helps to explain the phenomenon of civil society, which creates the space and shapes the institutional forms—including advocacy—for citizens to negotiate their interests with governments and, increasingly, with business, as with the fossil fuel industry, for example. In general, the more stable a state is, the more powerful it becomes. It's also why, in business in particular, innovation must often come from new enterprises, from entrepreneurs who have no stake in the status quo. But it can happen in established organizations as well, with the right leadership and mind-set.

Over the last 250 years, since the beginning of the Industrial Revolution, government- and business-led transformation have flourished together, marking an era of unprecedented growth and advancement for humankind. At their best, both means of promulgating change have reinforced each other, as when the government invented and regulated the Internet, while businesses scaled and disseminated it. Still, the imperative for transformative social progress remains, arguably more so than ever.

These two modes show two paths to transformation that are in many ways opposite. It can seem, then, that the job is to choose which path is called for in a given context and to proceed accordingly. Yet, in our complex world, there are challenges that are ill suited to either one of these modes. Business innovation produces some kinds of transformation well, and government policy innovation does others. Each has limits. But many imperatives sit in the space between the two modes. In these cases, actors have emerged who consciously seek to take elements from the two modes, bringing aspects of government and business-led transformation to the work of changing an equilibrium.

These new actors are taking different tacks and questioning assumptions in new ways. These actors seek to push society from a normal phase to revolution, and do so using whatever principles, structures, and tools they can to make the change most effectively. This emergent way forward, though not an entirely new force, has become more prominent over the last thirty years. It is social entrepreneurship.

Chapter 2

The Nature of Social Entrepreneurship

The 1970s were particularly tough years for Bangladesh. Monsoon floods and famine killed hundreds of thousands of people and devastated an already fragile economy. The country's poor villagers were hit hardest. But they were already locked into a cycle of unremitting poverty, with little opportunity to improve their livelihoods; even before devastating natural disasters, they suffered profoundly.

Among these were the citizens of Jobra, a small community in southwest Bangladesh, near Chittagong. There, a number of women eked out a subsistence wage making furniture. In order to make their stools and other items, the women needed supplies, especially bamboo. The trouble was, they didn't have the funds to buy those materials, leaving them no choice but to turn to exploitative middlemen. A middleman would provide the necessary supplies, but on the condition that the women sell their finished furniture back to him at a price he determined. These middlemen exerted complete control: they would provide enough materials for each stool and a few pennies for labor, then sell the stools at a tidy profit.

Obviously, if the women could have acquired their own materials and tools, they could have eliminated the middlemen and earned market rates for their furniture, vastly improving their lot. But options for acquiring the necessary supplies and capital were very limited. Notionally, funds could be procured from local moneylenders, but their rates were exorbitant and there was no way the women could generate enough profit to pay back such crushing debt. More formal banking services simply didn't exist for the poor in Jobra.

Shut out from access to the formal economy, villagers like the women of Jobra were born into poverty, worked their entire lives and raised their families in poverty, and died in poverty. They were, in effect, victimized by a very stable and very miserable equilibrium in which the power and resources were in the hands of others. It seemed there was little the women, or anyone else, could do to change the status quo.

Muhammad Yunus came to understand this cycle well. Yunus was a native Bangladeshi. A bright young man, he attended Dhaka University, earned a Fulbright Scholarship, and received a PhD in economics from Vanderbilt University. In the mid-1970s, he returned to Bangladesh and became head of the economics department at Chittagong University. As he explored nearby villages like Jobra, the pervasive poverty hit him hard, and he decided to take personal action.

But what action to take? Aid organizations had worked for decades to reduce the region's poverty, yet it remained endemic. Yunus chose a different approach. He began by seeking to understand the current context more deeply, delving into the scope and nature of the problem to be solved. The macroeconomic theories he taught didn't seem relevant.

Instead, he went to the people on the ground, asking a group of forty-two stoolmakers in Jobra how much money each would need to escape the middlemen and increase their productivity. Their answers added up to the equivalent of US $27. The sum shocked him. How could so small an amount stand between these hardworking women and a better future?

Yunus decided to run an experiment based on a new idea, an approach quite different than had had been tried by traditional aid programs and charities. He reached into his own pocket to lend the women the money they needed. He didn't really expect that they would repay it. But even so, this professor of economics made it a loan, rather than a charitable donation. As he explains: "When we want to help the poor, we usually offer them charity. Most often, we use charity to avoid recognizing the problem and finding the solution for it. Charity becomes a way to shrug off our responsibility. But charity is no solution to poverty. Charity only perpetuates poverty by taking the initiative away from the poor. Charity allows us to go ahead with our own lives without worrying about the lives of the poor. Charity appeases our consciences."[1] So his action was categorically not charity; to Yunus, it was business, albeit business with a social dimension. He was asking for repayment with interest. It was a risk, to be sure, but an entrepreneurial one.

His risk paid off. The women famously repaid every taka. With that, Yunus was prompted to think more deeply about the system that prevented these women from securing loans from nonpredatory sources. Conventional banking rules dictate that loans can be provided only where there is some guarantee, some collateral provided by the recipient. But the poorest of the poor have no collateral, making them unattractive candidates for conventional loans.

So Yunus began to formulate a new model, in which small loans could be made without relying on traditional forms of collateral from individual recipients. Loans would still be collateralized; otherwise, the risk to the lender would be too great. But the nature of the collateral was essentially different. The notion was to derisk individual loans by tying them to a larger community of recipients. The terms were strict but straightforward: "Loans were made to individuals but through small groups who in effect (if not explicitly) had joint liability; the loans were for business, not consumption; and collection was frequent, usually weekly. Interest charges were significant . . . but the rates were relatively low."[2]

This model became the foundation of Yunus's Grameen Bank (its name is derived from the Sanskrit word for *village*). Grameen would be the first venture of its kind, but it would not be the only such institution for long. The new model would ultimately spawn the microfinance industry, which has spread across the world and provided access to banking services and credit for hundreds of millions of poor customers. Although the origins of socially-oriented lending practices can be traced back centuries—and indeed Yunus was mentored by the founders of a US-based community development bank, Chicago's ShoreBank—Grameen Bank marked a seismic shift to broader and fairer credit access for the very poor.

All this began with looking at a long-standing problem in a new way. Yunus saw what others saw: that a lack of traditional collateral made the poor an unattractive risk for banks. But rather than accept the assumptions of the current equilibrium, Yunus recognized, as he is fond of saying that "all the ingredients for ending a person's poverty always [come] neatly packaged within that person."[3] Yunus realized he could collateralize the poor themselves by organizing them into guarantee-solidarity groups, in which members would back each other up, sharing the risk of individual default. His insight was to see this new form of collateral as the basis for an entirely new model of banking, one designed to lend tiny sums of money to the very poor.

Grameen Bank would go on to serve more than eight million customers, recovering more than 96 percent of its loans each year and earning over $250 million in revenue in 2010.[4] It would also, along with Yunus, win the 2006 Nobel Peace Prize, for "efforts to create economic and social development from below."[5]

Of course, not everyone was pleased with Grameen's success. Vested interests resisted, and eventually the Bangladeshi government removed Yunus from his position at the bank. And as enthusiasm for microcredit has grown, so have its critics and challengers, many of them questioning whether the model really does break the cycle of poverty. Yunus himself expresses concern over what his innovation has spawned, preferring to frame microcredit within a larger construct he calls "social business," whose purpose is not to generate returns for the wealthy, but to provide sustainable income generation capability to the poor. All the while, Grameen Bank remains active, and the transformation it catalyzed continues to expand.

Yunus clearly aimed at producing an equilibrium change in which the poverty of the furnituremakers, and millions in their position elsewhere, wasn't simply ameliorated, but transformed. Grameen Bank was a new kind of organization, and microcredit was a new mechanism for change. This story offers a quintessential example of social entrepreneurship, an example of equilibrium change that was neither purely government-led nor business-led transformation. Yunus borrowed thoughtfully, but liberally, from each—adapting principles and practices from the two modes to create an entirely new approach.

Business and government, as we've explored, are two forces that effect transformative change in profoundly different, even diametrically opposed ways. Transformation led by government and business proceeds in distinctive ways and along different dimensions, as illustrated in figure 2-1.

Two Forms of Transformation

Government-led transformation—innovation that seeks to dramatically, sustainably advance the state of society—has a set of specific attributes. First, the principal beneficiaries are citizens, those born under or naturalized into a given state and afforded specific rights and duties under its laws.

FIGURE 2-1

Dimensions of social transformation

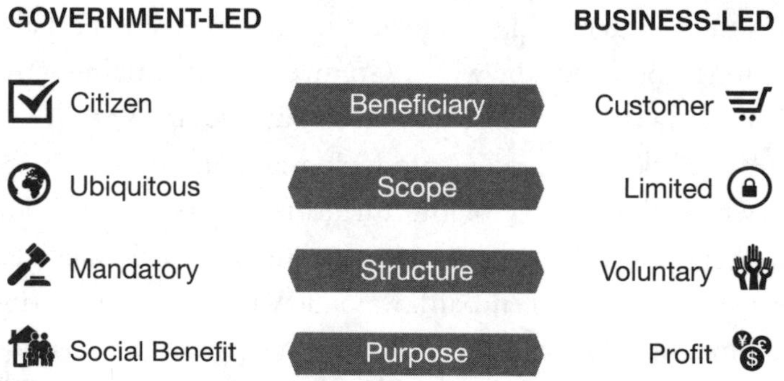

GOVERNMENT-LED		BUSINESS-LED
Citizen	Beneficiary	Customer
Ubiquitous	Scope	Limited
Mandatory	Structure	Voluntary
Social Benefit	Purpose	Profit

Government supports and is supported by its citizens, and its work aims to meet their needs.

Second, although some benefits of government action may accrue to individuals (politicians, for instance), government-led transformation is intended to be ubiquitous, spread across the broad spectrum of society. Even when a policy offers direct benefits toward a particular segment of society, as US civil rights legislation did in the 1960s, the rationale for the measure is that the broader society also benefits from the improved equilibrium—in this case, by living in a more fair and just world.

Third, the structure of the change driven by government policy change is typically mandatory. Through legislation and enforcement, a fundamental shift happens across the society, whether members of that society would choose to participate in that change voluntarily or not. Schools are integrated, health insurance is provided, and marriage laws are equalized. The equilibrium changes for all. While laws don't necessarily force citizens to do a particular thing (enter a same-sex marriage, for example), they apply to all citizens (a company can't deny benefits to same-sex partners even if it is not in favor of same-sex marriage).

The final dimension of transformation is the inherent purpose of the innovation, which in government-led transformation is social benefit: to improve society and move it forward. It isn't intended or designed to produce profit for some, but rather to produce benefit for all.

In contrast, business-led transformation is characterized by a different beneficiary, scope, structure, and purpose. The beneficiaries are customers, people who choose, of their own volition, to purchase a product or service from a company.

In business-led transformation, typically, the customer's life is made better through a fundamentally new product or service offering. Individuals are enabled, satisfied, or entertained in some new way.

Unlike government-led transformation, the effect is almost always limited in some way, rather than ubiquitous. Some customers avail themselves of the product or service, and some people don't. So the benefit does not automatically extend across the whole society. The offering isn't mandatory and enforced. The choice rests with the customer. This means, since there is no mandate or fiat, that a business must design its offerings to be attractive to customers and meet their needs.

Finally, there is no demand that all customers be served or treated equally, because the purpose of the enterprise isn't social benefit, but profit. Without profit, the business would cease to exist. This profit imperative does not diminish the fact that business-led transformation can advance the world, improve our standard of living, and make us better off. Think of the way in which the printing press, personal computers, mobile phones, or fluoride toothpaste, have made our lives better. Such business-led innovation transforms equilibriums.

This distinction between government and business as crucibles for societal change is not a matter of their different systems of governance or the kinds of institutions we associate with them. It's the structural and philosophical differences, aims, and intentions that are relevant here. Understanding how change proceeds from the two domains helps illuminate distinctive paths for those who seek to push the world forward. These paths are not, though, the only routes to change.

Social entrepreneurship offers a distinctive approach that borrows from these two modes in many different combinations.

Grameen Bank, for instance, produced neither a purely government-led nor a purely business-led transformation. Its products and services were offered voluntarily rather than under a broad mandate. It began as a limited offering, aimed squarely at the working poor in Bangladesh. As the equilibrium shifted, microcredit became much more ubiquitous. But Grameen plays only one part in that; it still has a limited base of customers and a limited reach. As with business-led transformation, Grameen's products and services were designed for a set of customers, not all citizens uniformly. But, as with a government-led effort, the goal was social benefit rather than profit—though in due course, when the new equilibrium was established, both social-benefit and for-profit players entered the space, helping to scale the solution and build out its sustaining ecosystem.

This form of equilibrium change is the sort of endeavor most of us associate with social entrepreneurship: a specific organization pursuing a social mission, sometimes operating with a double bottom line that attempts to balance profits with purpose. But this is only one form of social entrepreneurship. Modern social entrepreneurship takes many more forms. Its essence is found in its adaptive use of principles and practices from both government and business modes, often combining them in new ways.

Social entrepreneurship has grown up as an alternative way to tackle challenges that affect most citizens but do not easily conform to a mandated solution. It works on challenges that are effectively addressed through voluntary, limited organizational structures, but for which customers have little capacity to pay and little profit is possible. These kinds of challenges demand new models; they call on us to contest existing assumptions, and they encourage us to create new paths rather than follow the existing routes.

This fluid and adaptive approach distinguishes social entrepreneurs, no matter the specific legal structure or tax status of the organization in which they work or the domain of their pursuit. Ultimately, social entrepreneurship makes possible positive equilibrium-changing endeavors that do not fit neatly into the traditional modes of government and business. Businesses are constrained by the profit imperative and governments are constrained by the need for ubiquity of benefit. Social entrepreneurship negotiates these constraints.

The creative combination of elements from both poles—the government and business ends of the spectrum—is what enables social entrepreneurs to build models designed for a particular context, whether that context is a rural village in Bangladesh, well-appointed offices in the City of London, or the back rooms of India's sprawling bureaucracy. In each case, social entrepreneurs adapt what they need from the world of business and government. They work to tip society out of a normal phase to a new paradigm. They are social revolutionaries, even if they don't always look like it at first.

Sir Ronald Cohen and Big Society Capital

Take Sir Ronald Cohen. Bespectacled, slim, and impeccably dressed, Cohen cuts a dashing figure. He looks every inch a City of London man, which, of course, he is. Put plainly, his style and his résumé don't mark him out as a disrupter of the status quo. Born in Egypt, Cohen grew up just outside London. Despite beginning grammar school with just a few words of English at his disposal, Cohen went on to earn a scholarship to Oxford University. From there, he attended Harvard Business School and joined McKinsey & Company. In 1969, he cofounded Apax Partners, Britain's first private equity and venture capital firm, now operating with $20 billion in assets.

In many ways, Cohen is a prototypical entrepreneur. He and his partners set out with some seed capital to meet a need they saw in the world—lack of access to venture and equity funding. Driven by the opportunity to invest in new innovations, even in the face of inherent risks, Cohen built a significant and very profitable enterprise, to the benefit of his customers and himself.

Over his years at the helm of Apax, Cohen came to understand the potential and the limitations of business: "Entrepreneurship, innovation, and capital were extremely powerful levers for getting change made," he says. "At the social level, they certainly helped people from very diverse backgrounds to increase their wealth, the wealth of their communities, and the country more broadly. But they didn't close the gap between rich and poor. Basically, the gap between rich and poor grew bigger and bigger instead of smaller and smaller."[6]

Raised to believe in philanthropy as a way to address social needs, Cohen came to acknowledge its limitations too, particularly in tackling the persistent challenge of inequality. On its own, philanthropy was coming up short: "How do you begin to give real equality of opportunity to people, how do you help people get out of the difficult predicaments in which life had placed them?" he recalls asking. An answer eventually came: "I began to think of doing the same thing for social entrepreneurs as I'd been involved in doing for business entrepreneurs: connecting them to the capital markets, giving them the help to scale their organizations, think strategically about the future of their organizations, and achieve innovation."

The social sector, Cohen argued, wasn't as ineffective as is sometimes claimed. In fact, its results were often impressive, offering demonstrable benefits to society. But it did lack access to the range of capital options that would enable organizations to grow and scale. "There was no harnessing of entrepreneurship, capital, and innovation in the social sector," he says. "Even though the social sector is huge: In the United States, it is nine million people working in not-for-profits; it is three-quarters of trillion dollars of foundation assets. In the UK, it's eight hundred thousand people and about £100 billion of foundation assets. Yet the common characteristic is that everyone in the sector is small and nobody in the sector has any money."

The social sector's ability to build scale and attract resources, Cohen believed, was hampered by its lack of access to the capital markets. In business, entrepreneurs have access to multiple forms of capital to grow their enterprises: equity investment, secured debt, unsecured debt, and so on. In the social sector, by contrast, organizations depend in large part on charitable contributions and grants—both of which tend to be short-term in focus and often come with restrictions, especially on the amount of money that can be dedicated to administration. These restrictions can meaningfully hamper growth.

So Cohen started Big Society Capital in 2011 to provide social entrepreneurs access to capitalization avenues similar to those available to business entrepreneurs. "The role of Big Society Capital was that it should be a wholesaler of capital," he explains. "The purpose was to create social investment firms that would fund frontline social organizations in the not-for-profit sector." The firms that Big Society aims to create would provide secure debt, collateralized debt, or other capital instruments like social impact bonds, offering new options for the social sector similar to those that had long been used in business. "We're trying to show not-for-profits that they can build a balance sheet," Cohen says. "The balance sheet can have philanthropic capital at the bottom and then all the layers of capital sitting on top of that . . . It isn't really that different, in a way, in terms of entrepreneurship. You're backing entrepreneurs, giving them access to capital, except that their purpose is social."

To make it work, Cohen argues, the sector must develop credible metrics that can be correlated with financial returns, largely for governments but by extension to society at large. Calculating the true costs of social problems, then measuring the costs of interventions against them means organizations could quantify their impact in financial terms. "You can measure the performance of a not-for-profit organization," he says. "Since you can measure, you can link it to a financial return. If you can link the social performance to the financial return, then that's the key for a social entrepreneur to the capital markets." Social entrepreneurs must make a meaningful case for investment, he says, "not [just] having to go cap in hand to raise donations, but by saying, 'Look, I can deliver 7 percent to 10 percent uncorrelated returns. I can achieve social returns of more than double digits on improving the lives of prisoners, dropouts from school, homeless people, unemployed youth.'"

In building Big Society Capital, Cohen created a new model that drew from both government-led and business-led transformation to shift a social equilibrium. He saw that neither government nor business was well positioned to act alone: "I could see the limits of government ability to tackle an issue like the creation of jobs," he says. Companies were far better positioned to generate jobs through business innovation. Cohen has seen it firsthand at Apax: "As you look at the development of venture capital and the new technologies that it helped to fund, it completely transformed our lives. They've created sixty million jobs over twenty-five years, when fifty million were lost by smokestack industries. That has given me, going into impact investment, a sense that government can only do so much."

As an entrepreneur, Cohen brought the tools and mind-set of his line of work to an endeavor aimed at social benefit. "I think it's fair to say that, for me, social entrepreneurship is an extension of business entrepreneurship: the tools of business entrepreneurship had never been applied [to the social sector]."

Likely or not, Cohen is a revolutionary; he is working for social entrepreneurial transformation. It is early days, but his aim is to transform the way the social sector accesses capital. In this way, he wants to have ubiquitous impact, improving life for all citizens—but like Carnegie and Yunus, he has taken an entirely voluntary, customer-oriented approach, blending social impact and profit in new ways. Big Society Capital does not look to provide blanket funding for all social enterprises; it is a merit-based model, in which the best-performing organizations can grow and scale through access to the kinds of capital that fund business ventures. Cohen is building a model for achieving equilibrium change at scale, positioning his organization as an enabler for the broader sector. Big Society Capital takes direct action, providing funding to organizations that support frontline social service organizations and social entrepreneurs. It acts as an accelerator, helping to build the broad set of funding instruments and organizations that will scale and secure his innovative approach.

Cohen was able to see the possibilities in social finance, he says, because he came from outside the social sector. His venture capital expertise allowed him to see an opportunity missed by those on the inside, who were conditioned to the current equilibrium. It was this outsider's advantage that yielded his entrepreneurial insight: "It was really the power of investing, which I had witnessed firsthand in venture capital and private equity, being applied to battling social issues whose enormity required innovation and scale . . . You need to look at it as an outsider to understand it. If you're just within it, you just can't fathom it out." Cohen did fathom it and envisioned a better future—in which the social sector could access capital as efficiently as the private sector does. He built a model to effect that change and is working to scale it.

Cohen's particular area of focus (social impact investing) and the particular structure of his organization (operated by a trust, funded by £600 million from the UK Commission on Unclaimed Assets and a few hundred million pounds of equity from leading banks) are not the key determinants of whether Big Society Capital should be considered social entrepreneurship. Rather, it is that Cohen seeks to bring about equilibrium change and deploys principles and practices from both government- and business-led modes to achieve that goal. Along these dimensions, Cohen and his colleagues at Big Society can be considered social entrepreneurs.

Like Yunus, Cohen is not without his detractors. Some worry about shifting fundamental governmental responsibilities to the social sector. Others are skeptical about the structure of the instruments. They point to government's transfer of its risk to financial investors, who in turn, look to philanthropic investors to backstop their potential losses. Notwithstanding such critique, social finance, or what's being more broadly framed as *impact investing*, is an innovation conceived by social entrepreneurs aiming to drive social transformation through equilibrium change.

From examples like Big Society Capital and Grameen Bank, we can see how the tools and mind-set of entrepreneurship—of business-led transformation—can be mixed with aspects of government-led innovation to become social entrepreneurship. But social entrepreneurship is possible even within the halls of government itself, as Nandan Nilekani and his colleagues at the Unique Identification Authority of India demonstrate.

Unique Identification Authority of India (UIDAI) Project Aadhaar

Nandan Nilekani is one of India's most successful CEOs. He is also one its most transformative leaders. An engineer by training, Nilekani is one of the cofounders of Infosys, the IT services giant that helped spur India's technology revolution. He is even credited with telling author Thomas Friedman that the world is flat: Friedman links the thesis, and name, of his global best-seller to an interview with Nilekani, in which Nilekani made the case that the global playing field was leveling, that India and China were positioned to compete for work as never before.[7]

Nilekani has been called the Bill Gates of India. Technology and entrepreneurship form only part of the parallel. Like Gates, Nilekani has an appetite for a better world. After retiring from Infosys, Nilekani wrote a best-selling book on public policy. Published in 2008, *Imagining India* explored the contradictions inherent in the country that Nilekani loves.[8] Candid about its challenges and hopeful for what could be done to realize its potential, the book lays out ways India could capitalize on the opportunities it now has. One of Nilekani's ideas was the creation of a unique identifier for individuals. He believed it could address one of the most pervasive challenges facing India's poorest citizens: securing their personal identification.

It seems hard to fathom. In the West, most children are born in hospitals, where they are automatically issued a birth certificate. That piece of paper, Nilekani explains, "becomes the building document on which you get your citizenship."[9] Without this proof of identification, individuals are unable to claim their legal rights. They aren't permitted to drive, vote, or legally work. They can't gain straightforward access to government services. They can't open a bank account or apply for a loan. Absent identification documents, they are effectively considered nonpersons, cut off from most economic activity and from the chance to exercise their rights as citizens.

This, believe it or not, was the case for an estimated four hundred million people in India just a decade ago. Contemplate that scale: more people in India lacked formal documents than live in the whole of the United States. This was an unhappy state of affairs, but it was also an equilibrium. Those who lacked documentation were typically poor, and their very lack of documentation made it almost impossible to effectively change the system. In technical terms, they were nonpersons, with no influence on or participation in the formal legal and economic systems that represented the status quo.

In *Imagining India*, Nilekani had pointed out this dire equilibrium and proposed a solution to shift it. His idea was to provide every one of India's 1.2 billion citizens a unique, fraud-proof identifier. In 2009, a year after the book's publication, then prime minister Manmohan Singh asked Nilekani to turn the idea into reality. Singh appointed Nilekani chairman of an agency working on the same challenge, the Unique Identification Authority of India (UIDAI), which was running an ID project called Project Aadhaar (the Hindi work for foundation or base). With that, the entrepreneur became a bureaucrat.

But the entrepreneur would not be easily co-opted. Nilekani was really in the game of applying the tools and principles of business-led transformation to achieve social good, aiming to drive an equilibrium shift that would leave his country positively transformed. As he saw it, with a unique identifier program, not only would India's poor gain identity and access to civic benefits, but also the country's burden of welfare fraud would be reduced. In the end, he believed, India could leapfrog Western nations in the scope and security of its identification tools.

As Nilekani explains, "At one level, you can think of [the unique ID project] as one of the world's largest social inclusion projects. That's one part of what it tries to solve. The second thing that it's trying to solve is common to all societies that build welfare programs. When you build a welfare program in any society, you need a way to identify your residents, so that (a) you can make sure the benefits will go to the right person, and (b) [you can ensure] that the same person can be identified over time." With so many of India's poor lacking identification, social programs were ripe for fraud and misuse. A unique identifier would enable welfare and other support services to go to those who were really in need—and to those who really were who they said they were. "On one hand, you are solving an issue of social inclusion by giving everyone an ID to participate in society, and on the other hand, you are making government expenditure on welfare more efficient, more effective, and more equitable," Nilekani explains.

Ever the integrative thinker—unwilling to choose between the best interests of individuals and of the government—Nilekani seized on the opportunity to do both, through the same initiative. He knew, of course, it wouldn't be easy. Getting started was a hurdle. The poor had no base documents, no way to prove their identity in the first place. So the initial challenge was to address that deficiency. "We had to have a fairly foolproof way of establishing uniqueness," Nilekani explains.

Fortunately, in the face of global security threats, governments and businesses around the world were making great strides in using biometrics to establish uniqueness—leveraging fingerprints, eye scans, and so on. "After a little bit of research and proof of concept, we came to the conclusion that if you do multimodal biometrics, combining the irises of both eyes and the fingerprints of all ten fingers, the digital signature—the digital pattern of these—is unique across a billion people." This approach enabled the agency to assess new registrants against its database to ensure their biometric patterns were not duplicates. It could do so with an accuracy of over 99.9 percent.

The basic strategy was to provide every citizen who registered with a unique twelve-digit identifier tied to his or her specific biometric pattern. This number could be verified when needed, using the biometric identifiers. It would provide individuals with access to government services and enable them to claim the rights of citizenship. But, importantly, the identifier could be used far beyond voting and government programs. In banking, for instance, companies could use the identifier to verify a customer's identity. This means that the identifier promised value for a broad cross-section of citizens, even if the primary and greatest benefit was conferred to the very poor.

Given the scope of the problem, Nilekani knew he needed a large-scale solution. Fast, efficient, and effective implementation would be critical to producing sustainable change. So he designed an ecosystem of partners—outside agencies and organizations that could act as registrars using UIDAI's software. He explains that "the state government, banks and post offices . . . all of them could act as registrars. At peak, we had more than thirty thousand such enrollment stations across the country . . . UIDAI was doing more than one million unique IDs a day."

Nilekani and his team designed with scale and efficiency in mind from the outset: "Scalability at the back end through technology, scalability at the front end through technology and process, and a business model that allowed multiple organizations to become enrolling agencies . . . There were more than a hundred thousand people in our ecosystem, but only three hundred people in the main organization," he says with a hint of pride. "Like the brain of the system, it is a highly leveraged model, where a small set of people design the technology, the solution, the business model."

Nilekani also thought carefully through the implications of the capital and operating expenditures of a program of this size, anxious to avoid crippling start-up costs and overwhelming capital risk for the agency as the technology was built out across the country. So UIDAI developed a model by which enrolling agencies purchased the enrolling equipment and were then reimbursed a small amount for every ID issued. This brought down the UIDAI's capital costs and distributed risk across the ecosystem. It made the system scalable and robust over time.

By 2014, when Nilekani stepped down as chairman, more than 720 million people had been issued their unique twelve-digit Aadhaar number. The number is expected to reach one billion by 2016.[10] Again, the program is not without its critics—some of whom raise privacy concerns or question the decision to provide the number to residents as well as citizens. But its impact is very real: 720 million registrants, tied to sixty million bank accounts, and more than one hundred agencies using the identifier for authentication.[11]

UIDAI looks at first like standard government-led transformation. The originating agency, for starters, was set up as a branch of government. Its chairman was officially a civil servant holding a cabinet-level position. Its employees are all civil servants, and UIDAI reported directly to the government. In addition, recipients are not charged for their identification card; as such, the model conforms to the typical free government service, designed for ubiquity and social benefit.

But other aspects are utterly unlike traditional government-led efforts. Nilekani ran the Authority in the spirit of an entrepreneurial venture—with a small team supported by an extensive network of partners. He built a platform on which enterprises could create for-profit applications. These services made it attractive for all Indians to enroll, not just the rural poor. This was an important part of the puzzle, because unlike traditional government entitlements secured by legislation, no fiat was involved here. Enrollment is a purely voluntary activity, just as customers choose to avail themselves of a product or service offered by the private sector. Here, the beneficiaries can be conceived of as both citizens and as customers, depending on when and how they use their Aadhaar number. In the end, UIDAI simply cannot be pegged as either business- or government-led transformation; it is a classical expression of social entrepreneurship, making Nandan Nilekani a social entrepreneur—even within a traditional government space. So we see social entrepreneurship operating in different manners, taking on different organizational structures, and spanning different time frames as befits a specific purpose.

Ways and Means

It is fair to say that our world moves ahead in fits and starts as we struggle to make societies more just and the world a happier place. Most of the time, our advances are of the normal science variety: somebody figures out a way to make the current equilibrium just a little bit better. It might be a business that tweaks its product or service to the benefit of users. It might be a government that alters a piece of legislation to produce a new benefit for society. It might be a social service provider that figures out a way to ameliorate the pain and suffering of those for whom the existing equilibrium is particularly miserable. These incremental advances are helpful, and the governments, businesses, and other organizations that work to produce them deserve our encouragement and support.

But big, positive changes are vital to transforming equilibriums. Such shifts happen infrequently and episodically, but they make a disproportionate difference to the fate of our world. Governments have a long track record of producing these equilibrium shifts through policy innovation, often in response to the dogged work of far-seeing and effective social activists. Businesses have a shorter but equally important track record in producing positive equilibrium shifts through their innovations as well, motivated by both profit and by the opportunity to provide something to the world that had never before been offered before. As two principal modes of social transformation, government- and business-led transformation have been implemented for centuries. Now, though, there is an alternative mode for approaching equilibrium change.

Social entrepreneurship is a much newer source of positive social change; its activities and models navigate the extensive territory between the modes of business-led and government-led transformation. Although still nascent, social entrepreneurship's early results point to a promising future, in large part because of its ability to draw on and combine key features from the crucibles of business and government innovation, an ability that promises almost unlimited potential and many ways forward.

At the heart of the equilibrium transformation is a unique model that social entrepreneurs design for their particular context. It could be a new financial service for the very poor. It could be a model for providing access to multiple forms of capital funding to social-sector players. Or it could help non-identified individuals claim citizenship status in their own country. In each case, the model is new to the world and changes a stable but unhappy equilibrium as it brings about a new, better one.

How do they do it? So far, we have seen that social entrepreneurs dip into the playbooks of both business-led and government-led transformation to create a powerful and potent combination. But how do they actually go about it? How do social entrepreneurs see the problem, conceive a solution, build a model for change, and scale it? These are the questions to which we will turn in part II.

Part II

Paths to Transformation

Chapter 3

Understanding the World

In her book *Cinderella's Sisters: A Revisionist History of Footbinding*, historian Dorothy Ko begins with the story of a most unusual donation. In 1999, the Heilongjiang Museum of Ethnography in Harbin, China, received eight pairs of tiny wooden shoe lasts from the Zhiqiang Shoe Factory. The forms, the smallest of which was just three inches in length, had been used by the factory's aging craftsmen to fashion dainty lotus shoes, the delicate embroidered footwear worn by women who'd had their feet bound as girls. The company had been selling just a few hundred pairs of the tiny shoes per year, mainly to women in their eighties and nineties. With this donation, the company formally ceased all production of lotus shoes, closing the book on a practice that had lasted almost a thousand years. The significance of the moment was not lost on the museum staff. In a ceremonial acceptance of the lasts, Heilongjiang's curator called the three-inch golden lotus "an historical testament to thc bodily and psychological damage that women suffered in feudal society. The sad songs of small feet would never be sung again."[1] The end of foot binding marked a truly seismic shift in Chinese society.

Believed to have originated in the ninth or tenth century in the Emperor's court, foot binding was the practice of applying tight wraps to young girls' feet to prevent the feet from growing. The process would begin when a girl was five or six years old, when the bones of the feet were still pliable. Documentarian Amanda Foreman explains:

> First, her feet were plunged into hot water and her toenails clipped short. Then the feet were massaged and oiled before all the toes, except the big toes, were broken and bound flat against the sole, making a triangle shape. Next, her arch was strained as the foot was bent double. Finally, the feet were bound in place using a silk strip measuring ten feet long and two inches wide. These wrappings were briefly removed every two days to prevent blood and pus from infecting the foot. Sometimes "excess" flesh was cut away or encouraged to rot. The girls were forced to walk long distances in order to hasten the breaking of their arches. Over time the wrappings became tighter and the shoes smaller as the heel and sole were crushed together.[2]

The process must have been excruciating. But the tiny feet that resulted were considered a mark of sophistication and status. A woman with perfect "lotus feet" became the standard of beauty, and foot binding became a prerequisite for a woman to marry well. Efforts to ban the practice began as early as the 1600s, but foot binding remained the norm across most of China. It was a strong, stable equilibrium that government edicts and well-intentioned missionary projects would fail to shift for the next four hundred years.

Then, that equilibrium changed, ending the practice in the course of a single generation. British philosopher and cultural theorist Kwame Anthony Appiah argues that the shift was the result not of simple government action or pure social advocacy, but of a national movement for change fueled by "a mixture of campaigning outsiders and modernizing insiders"—Chinese nationals and Anglo-European expatriate residents.[3] The individuals and organizations who brought an end to the practice had taken stock of a stable but unhappy equilibrium—one in which millions of girls were subjected to torture in pursuit of an ancient ideal—that was deeply rooted in society. But they believed it was changeable, and they built institutions to effect that change. Their first step: a commitment to deeply understanding the culture, context, and traditions that enabled the current equilibrium to thrive.

Why Understand?

For the social entrepreneur, an intensive understanding of a particular status quo propels all that follows. In order to intervene in an existing equilibrium, one must first recognize it for what it is: a condition established over time and held in place by members of the society who take its existence, and their role in perpetuating it, largely for granted. If the mothers binding their daughters' feet questioned what they were doing, the pressures of the status quo were strong enough to force acquiescence. The mothers did what had been done to them, carrying on a practice that they understood would assure their daughters' status in Chinese society.

Calling attention to the practice—labeling it barbaric and its adherents benighted—had not been effective at changing the long-entrenched equilibrium. Nor had government edicts. To chart the path to change, to spur a new equilibrium, those working to end foot binding had to engage in a new way. For instance, they had to understand the way in which foot binding had become tied not just to standards of beauty, but also to notions of Chinese identity. In other words, they needed to begin with the existing equilibrium and understand it fully—charting its actors, their roles, and the reinforcing dynamics of their interactions—in order to have a hope of transforming the system.

The point is fundamental. Most of us don't set out to change the world; rather, we proceed along prescribed lines, setting ourselves to the task of mastering the rules of a given milieu. Students who hope to succeed at university know they must follow the professor's syllabus, carry out assignments, and study for tests. Physicians working within Kuhn's "normal science" construct don't question whether dietary fat is to blame for a patient's high blood pressure: they simply prescribe statins and put the patient on a low-fat regimen. Chinese parents who want their daughters to be accepted in society bind their daughters' feet. Human beings largely accept the world as it is; we figure out its rules, terms, and conditions, focusing our energies on maximizing our performance within them. Even if we wish the world were different, we rarely move to change it. Instead, we tread the path that's laid out and familiar, and we show the way for others to follow.

This is the powerful social inertia that social entrepreneurs question. When they see an unjust equilibrium, they don't settle into acquiescence. They may well start out where most of us do, tacitly accepting "what is." But before long, that perspective undergoes a dramatic transformation as the social entrepreneur seeks to understand the problem in a new way. He or she deliberately sets out to make sense of the problematic equilibrium itself: how did it come to be and why does it persist?

At its heart, this process of understanding is a paradoxical exercise. Social entrepreneurs must navigate three powerful tensions in understanding the world they wish to change: abhorrence and appreciation; expertise and apprenticeship; and experimentation and commitment. To understand the world, and to have a chance of changing an equilibrium, social entrepreneurs must navigate their own perceptions of a given status quo, abhorring its outcomes on the one hand and appreciating how it works on the other. As they proceed, they must draw on what they know and recognize what they do not yet understand, shifting between leveraging their own expertise and apprenticing with others. And finally, they must act, alternately experimenting in order to test out possible interventions for change and committing to what works as the experiments pile up.

Throughout this process, social entrepreneurs must ensure that they don't tilt toward one extreme or the other for too long. Active negotiation of opposing ways of thinking and acting is key to understanding the world enough to change it. Disciplined and agile inquiry is required to get to the bottom of how any equilibrium has come to be and the reasons for its tenacious hold. Taken together, these efforts can produce a profound level of understanding, the necessary precondition for social entrepreneurial success. For many of the social entrepreneurs we have studied, these appear to be ways of thinking and proceeding taken implicitly; the process leading to eventual success seems more intuitive than intentional. But, even if social entrepreneurs could not at first have articulated the path they chose, we are able to see distinctive patterns in what they did and how they did it. Take Molly Melching, who has spent her life working to change a deeply rooted equilibrium in Africa.

Understanding Senegal

In 1974, Molly Melching arrived in Senegal, thrilled to be embarking on what was to be a six-month academic adventure. Twenty-four years old, she had been selected for an exchange program with the University of Dakar, one of two graduate students from the University of Illinois. Within hours of landing, however, Melching learned that the program had been canceled. Undeterred, she found temporary housing with the US embassy and "simply began showing up" at the university every day. "I can't leave," she told officials. "I'm here. We need to make this work."[4] Her persistence paid off. In due course, she convinced university officials to honor the terms of their original agreement. She was given a place in the master's program, a $50-a-month stipend, and a room in the women's dorm.

She had come to Dakar to deepen her knowledge of French colonialism, believing that the experience of living and studying in Senegal would enrich her perspective on her work. But

Melching's interest in French literature would soon wane. Instead, she fell in love with Senegal and its people. "The people are so kind and generous, warm and affectionate," she says. "Their welcome, as they say, the *teraanga*, just gets in your blood."[5]

Senegal drew Melching in. Accepting a job as a translator for development agencies, she began heading out from the urban familiarity of Dakar, with its French enclaves of cafés and bookstores, into rural villages. There, she was confronted by a stark reality: hungry children, contaminated water, illness, and suffering. She watched as Western development agencies tried, and failed, to effect change. Nothing seemed to alter the prevailing dynamic.

The First Tension: Abhorrence and Appreciation

The drive of change agents, including social entrepreneurs, is often ignited by their feeling that something has gone horribly wrong. But objection to a particular status quo, no matter how strongly expressed, is rarely enough to make a difference. Why? All too often, in the face of an unjust equilibrium, we fall prey to the instinct to reject the current state entirely. But a visceral rejection of an all-powerful system tilts completely to abhorrence, making it difficult to engage with the system deeply enough to see the levers for change.

In fact, whole-cloth rejection of an all-powerful system can often have the effect of reinforcing the system we aim to change. Those who most benefit from the status quo, who accept its terms and play by its rules, will burrow more deeply within it when faced with fierce and vocal opposition. The current equilibrium feels to them certain and unchangeable. It is just the way things are—and it is the way it is for a reason; accordingly, advocates for change can be seen as both delusional and dangerous. Those who most appreciate the current equilibrium, in other words, may be least likely to want to change it. Yet it is often those most deeply inside the system who can articulate its mechanisms—how and why it works as it does. They have the access required to appreciate and understand the system.

It is a tricky paradox, then. Those most angered by what they see as an unjust equilibrium typically find it all but impossible to engage deeply with the status quo they loathe. Those inside it can understand it, but see little reason or opportunity to change it. The most successful change agents, by contrast, must manage to both abhor the existing conditions and appreciate the system that produces them, deeply and well. They must truly understand how and why an equilibrium works, while remaining steadfast in their mission to shift it. This balance is extremely hard to maintain because it is a balance of a particularly dynamic type. There can be no perfectly set position between fiercely despising and deeply inquiring; rather, successful social entrepreneurs must employ a disciplined process for toggling back and forth between the extremes.

It is this active exercise that starts to generate meaningful understanding. As social entrepreneurs discover how the current equilibrium has come to exist and what holds it in place, they equip themselves to design transformational solutions. Without such comprehensive understanding, would-be social entrepreneurs will remain actors within the existing system or outsiders looking in. They will fail to achieve transformation. Without a balance between appreciation and abhorrence, they are likely to seek to ameliorate rather than transform a miserable condition, to rush to what seems an obvious but simplistic answer, to overlook some fatal flaw in an appealing idea, or to fixate on a single influential interest or actor rather than the ecosystem—all common actions that fall short of equilibrium change.

In her first few years in Africa, Melching found herself engaging ever more deeply with two worlds—the vibrant communities of Senegal and the Western development agencies that sought to improve conditions in the region. In her work, as she dutifully translated what development officials had to say to poor villagers, she was struck by the one-sided nature of the exchange: "There was little true dialogue happening, no deep inquiry into what was working for villagers and what they thought should be changed. I kept waiting for a conversation to happen, but it rarely did."[6]

Armed with their plans for new water wells, schools, and millet grinders, development officials explained their projects and the benefits expected to accrue to communities. Questions were not asked; opinions were not solicited. Nor was any provision for educating villagers about the ongoing management of such aid projects part of the program. The international development agencies and their hardworking staffs were not ill intentioned; they clearly abhorred and sought to ameliorate the bleak conditions they encountered. But, sadly, their interventions met with little success, because the development community largely failed to appreciate why the equilibrium they faced was so pervasive and so stable.

Aid work was then and largely continues to be rooted in a powerful ideology that took shape in the wake of World War II. As industrialized countries of the West invested in rebuilding their economic engines, technology dominated. Technological innovation had been essential to winning the war and it now promised to pay significant dividends to post-war economies in the West. At the same time, there was a recognition that America's prewar isolationism could not continue in the face of an emerging postcolonial, interconnected, and interdependent global economy. To prevent the kinds of economic upheaval that had led to the war and to fend off the growing threat of Marxism, America and its Western allies would engage in a new way with the developing world, using a technology-aided development approach to bolster the global economy and seed capitalism around the world.

Structural adjustment programs, as they came to be known, began to dominate development through the 1950s. Creditor nations increasingly insisted on loan terms that required recipients to move toward more capitalistic and industrialized models. Aid programs were steeped in these same capitalist principles, offering the promise of transformative technology on terms set by the West.

Although Melching didn't fully know it at the time, the development officers she accompanied into Senegal's rural outposts were schooled in this system, trained to implement utilitarian technologies in poor countries without much regard—much less respect—for the cultural context of the current equilibrium.

Dennis Whittle was a product of that system. As a development economist, he worked in Asia and Africa in the

1980s and 1990s, first with the Asian Development Bank and USAID, and then with the World Bank. Looking back on his experience, Whittle is blunt in his assessment:

> The mental model in the development community when I began working in the field in 1984 was very top-down and expert-driven, and went as follows: The developing world suffers from a severe shortage of both know-how and money. Official aid agencies such as the World Bank, the UN, and bilateral aid agencies need to aggregate the world's best expertise and money—and then deliver them to poorer countries. At that time, there was also a growing number of nongovernmental organizations (NGOs). Though they get money from different sources (from donors rather than taxpayers), in practice, many NGOs operate with a similar mind-set: "We know what people need, we know how to deliver it, and we are here to give it to them."[7]

Even at this early stage, Melching struggled against the mind-set Whittle describes. Everywhere she turned, she saw the signs of failed development initiatives: corroded machines, empty buildings, and broken water pumps.[8] Working within the traditional development world, Melching saw how this approach worked, and how it didn't work. Essentially, it tilted to abhorrence. It took an approach that said: a specific current equilibrium in Africa is unacceptable, and we will change it with technology from the outside. There was little appreciation of the reasons indigenous communities operated as they did, why the unhappy equilibriums that prevailed in Africa persevered even in the face of new incentives. Melching came to believe that a different approach was necessary if change was to happen sustainably in Senegal: "True social change—true development—seems possible only when you work with the people," she reflects, "when you start with where they are, and with their input, consider what needs to change."[9]

So Melching sought to engage ever more deeply with communities in Senegal—to learn from and build relationships with village elders and young people, to explore community networks, and to shape her knowledge of how the society was structured. She came to see the power of the deeply interconnected community structures and the way in which they tied individuals tightly together. She saw the influence of elders and religious leaders, as well as the supportive and close-knit networks of women within each village. She noted the joy with which the Senegalese celebrated life's gifts and the way in which music and dance were knitted into the life of a community. She experienced how long-held traditions were passed on from father to son, and mother to daughter. She came to appreciate just how a community was structured and the norms under which it operated. But even as she sought to appreciate and understand, she continued to abhor—not the Senegalese people and their practices, but the equilibrium that kept them in profound and abject poverty, despite a near-constant flow of aid dollars and development projects.

Melching came to understand the ways in which village networks and community structures could reinforce the existing equilibrium by maintaining a deeply held dynamic: a fundamental inequality between the sexes, in which women were considered to be entirely subservient to men, first to their fathers and then to their husbands. The profound disempowerment of women, she believed, fed and reinforced the cycle of poverty. But it was deeply rooted in the status quo.

This dynamic, she learned from her friend, a traditional healer named Daouda Ndiaye, was based in legend, passed from generation to generation. The first woman and man on earth, the story went, were asked by the Great Spirit what they wanted of life. The woman desired to be the master of the world, to have dominion over it. The canny man then chose to be master of the woman. This was the reason, then, that women suffered in childbirth (and required by custom to do so in silence). It was why women were bound to honor and obey their husbands and fathers. It was why women had been, and remained, under the rule of men.

It was also the reason for the traditional practice of female genital cutting, the initiation rite representing the passage from childhood to womanhood. This procedure entails the removal of a girl's external genitalia, and is traditionally performed to ensure her social acceptance, religious adherence, chastity, and/or marriageability. The practice is widespread across western, eastern, and northeastern Africa, from Somalia to Senegal, with some 125 million girls and women around the world today having been subject to the mutilation.[10] Female genital cutting is responsible for long-term health problems, including recurrent infections, infertility, reduced sexual enjoyment, and increased risk of complications in childbirth.

Stumbling into a female genital cutting ceremony for the first time, in the Casamance region of southern Senegal, Melching saw an arresting sight: twenty teenaged girls sitting on the ground in a straight line, legs stretched out to touch the back of the girl in front. Dressed in traditional garb, with beads draped along their foreheads and faces painted white, the girls were silent as they prepared to begin a painful month-long process of cutting, treatment, and healing. When it was complete, they would be ready for marriage. Some of the girls were as young as twelve years old.

Melching saw female genital cutting not as an isolated issue, but as one feature of a system that subjugated women—the norms within each community that stopped women from insisting on change and the way in which the community enforced those norms through social and economic incentives. A woman who stepped outside her accepted role or who refused to have her daughter cut could be beaten or ostracized, see her children rejected by her community, and find her financial supports removed.

To reach this in-depth understanding, Melching needed to toggle between seeking to understand the system—appreciating and considering its dynamics—and seeking to change it. She had to negotiate the relationship between the dispassionate inquiry that comes from appreciation and the passionate conviction that comes from abhorrence. She had to prepare herself to use her existing expertise while apprenticing to extend it. This is the next tension social entrepreneurs navigate: they assume familiar and unfamiliar roles, roles that build on what they know and invite them to discover what they don't. By taking on these opposing roles, social entrepreneurs set themselves up to discover and adapt, which steels them to the long-term, not-for-the-faint-of-heart work of equilibrium change.

The Second Tension: Expertise and Apprenticeship

Expertise plays an unexpectedly important role in the process of understanding. In fact, many social entrepreneurs come to their work of transformation as experts in a specific domain. Think back to Muhammad Yunus. He is an economist, which enabled him to understand how the moneylending system in place prevented the poor from advancing. Ronald Cohen is a venture capitalist, which helped him to see that the social sector lacked access to the kinds of capital that enable growth and scale in the business world. Vicky Colbert is a trained educator with a focus on the sociology of education, which enabled her to understand why education in rural schools was delivered as it was and to imagine how it might be delivered differently. Similarly, Melching's proficiency in the French and Wolof languages helped her pick up the nuances of both colonial and indigenous dimensions of Senegalese culture. In her work as a translator for Western agencies, she also became attuned to the language of development and sensitive to its dissonant notes.

Expertise in a specific domain can be vital for social entrepreneurs, helping them understand the system dynamics of a current equilibrium in a new way or to identify what is missing or misaligned in a social system. But expertise alone is not sufficient for in-depth understanding and equilibrium change. Expertise may very well set the social entrepreneur on her journey and equip her to see what others miss, but it is only a starting point. Expertise can be a trap in which we see the world from a single perspective. The development and aid workers Melching had encountered were experts too—but often, experts allow their domain-specific knowledge to dominate their understanding of the world. Social entrepreneurs understand that expertise must be balanced with naïveté, a willingness to see the world from a very different vantage point—that of the apprentice.

Contextual immersion is often key to this process. As social entrepreneurs look to build out their understanding, they will purposefully gravitate to new and unfamiliar experiences. Yunus explored the villages around his home and spoke with the villagers, seeking to understand their perspectives and to see the problem through their eyes. Nandan Nilekani entered the civil service, where he had to navigate new ways of operating and new ways of engaging, constructing new systems that could work with existing ones to serve India's citizens rather than Infosys's customers.

The social entrepreneur will also learn to draw on the wisdom of those not seen or classified as experts, especially those living within the system, in order to gain insights about their beliefs and practices. Instead of deferring to the prevailing wisdom embraced by those who benefit from the status quo, of whom he may well be one, the social entrepreneur positions himself to absorb lessons from ecosystem actors, especially those most disadvantaged by the existing equilibrium. Melching's immersion in Senegalese culture brought her into contact with both experts and "nonexperts," but especially with the people of Senegal. She sought out mentors from all walks of life—from revered African historian Cheikh Anta Diop to traditional healers to Western educators—in order to balance out what she knew about development and language. But mainly, Melching came to know the people of Senegal—the women of the villages—as friends and teachers.

She began to apprentice herself to them, seeking to understand how they navigated the social systems in their villages, how they influenced others, and how they inspired change within the system.

She came to see that existing education initiatives, in particular, were less effective than they could be because they failed to take context into account. Upon first arriving in Dakar, Melching had volunteered at a city orphanage, where she was dismayed to find most of the books and other materials were woefully inappropriate, vestiges of French colonialism with no relevance to the lives and culture of Senegal's children. What was the sense of an educational system that insisted on carrying out all public instruction in French, when villagers spoke Wolof or another indigenous language? How helpful were Western books that offered no connection to Senegalese culture and traditions in inspiring children to read? From these questions, Melching formed an intention to act—not yet to change the inequality equilibrium, for she hadn't created a model for that yet—but to do something, to take action personally and directly.

Just as negotiating the tension between appreciation and abhorrence provides the spark that sets the social entrepreneur on the path to learn more, alternately donning the hats of expert and apprentice enables him to see what others don't, and to delve ever deeper into the nature of the existing equilibrium. Each role tests and expands the lessons gained from the other. And because each role also carries the same risk—that of becoming acculturated to the status quo—the real trick is in the movement between them to avoid being co-opted by what is. Then, as Melching shows us, the social entrepreneur must do more than think about the equilibrium—she must act, but again, in a particular and distinctive way that balances a third tension: experimentation and commitment.

The Third Tension: Experimentation and Commitment

Social entrepreneurs feel confident in their understanding of the world, but also recognize that there is much they don't know. Rather than being paralyzed by the significant gaps in their knowledge, they design and run experiments to fill in these gaps. The most successful social entrepreneurs demonstrate a willingness to question assumptions and a resilience that prevents them from being devastated when those assumptions turn out be invalid. They know that the only way to really learn about the world, and certainly the best way to learn how to change it, is to test and experiment in that world.

Again, though, an experimental mode must be balanced with another, opposing mode: deep commitment. The successful social entrepreneur does not flit from one approach to another, forever playing with new ideas. She does not experiment randomly, but rather does so with sustained commitment to shifting an equilibrium. She uses experiments to build up knowledge and to enable commitment to the ones that prove out in practice. She does this because to actually bring about equilibrium change, social entrepreneurs have to commit to a course of action and drive an idea to fruition. Absent such dedication, there will be no scaling and no transformed equilibrium. Finally, this toggling between experimentation and commitment is not a one-time effort.

Successful social entrepreneurs will continue to experiment within the committed course, striving to improve their chances of achieving equilibrium change.

Melching experimented long and hard. She began with the idea of creating more effective teaching materials for the children she had met in Dakar. She wrote an illustrated children's book, *Anniko!*, in the Wolof language, encouraging local Senegalese artists and writers to do the same. Next, she approached Peace Corps officials with the idea of instructing children in Wolof. The proposal was initially rebuffed: "I'm not saying any of this is a bad idea, but maybe you don't understand how the Peace Corps works," came the response. "I know exactly how it works," Melching shot back. "But can't we make it work a little differently this time?" Eventually, the officials relented, and Melching launched Demb ak Tey ("Yesterday and Today") from two rooms in the popular African Cultural Center, located in the Medina, among Dakar's poorest and most densely populated neighborhoods. There, she experimented with new ways of engaging with the community, new subjects of instruction, and new methods of teaching.

By 1991, Melching was ready to commit to an approach. She founded Tostan (the name means "breakthrough" in Wolof) to scale a Community Empowerment Program (CEP), comprising six learning models: problem-solving skills, health and hygiene, financial management for village projects, leadership and group dynamics, and planning for income-generating projects. Literacy and numeracy were integral to all modules. Participating communities were required to house a Tostan facilitator for the program's three-year duration, to provide a place for classes to meet, and to establish a community management committee (made up of seventeen members, at least eight of them women) who would coordinate activities and manage any projects emerging from class discussion. Villagers were equipped, in other words, to plan and carry out projects that would benefit their communities, rather than remaining dependent on development agencies to deliver aid projects to them. This, Melching believed, could shift the poverty cycle if deployed at scale.

Three years later, Tostan's CEP was reaching fifteen thousand participants in 350 villages. External evaluations found that Tostan's program had succeeded in achieving its goals: villagers learned to read and write, they understood and could address the causes of common childhood illnesses, and they showed greater ability to resolve issues affecting their communities. Word of Tostan's results spread, prompting UNESCO to name the organization "one of the most innovative non-formal education programs in the world."[11]

Melching wasn't done. While CEP had the potential to impact the unhappy equilibrium—the development approach that disenfranchised those whom it aimed to help—she continued to struggle with a piece of the puzzle she had not yet fully addressed: the mistreatment and marginalization of women. To get to the root of the problem, Melching toggled back to the appreciative apprentice role; she carried out hundreds of interviews, all of which reinforced what she observed to be a pervasive acceptance by women of their lot:

> Women were so accustomed to being mistreated and so often the victims of discrimination that they didn't believe they were worthy of any other treatment. What they needed was not just closer hospitals or better-trained medical workers, but a way of envisioning an alternative

existence in which they understood their right to be treated with dignity. It was only if they believed they were entitled to better treatment that they could demand it.[12]

Melching saw a way she might help the women of Senegal to envision that better equilibrium when she learned that Senegal had ratified the UN's Convention on the Elimination of All Forms of Discrimination Against Women in 1985. The Convention focused on three key areas: civil rights, reproductive rights, and gender relations. It affirmed the equal rights of women and men in regard to all familial matters and required that ratifying nations confront social and cultural practices enabling gender discrimination. Even stronger prohibitions against violence toward women became international law eight years later, when the UN ratified the Declaration on the Elimination of Violence Against Women, guaranteeing women's freedom from physical, sexual, and psychological violence, including domestic abuse, dowry-related brutality, and marital rape.

In these declarations, Melching found a way in. She could use them to start a conversation in villages about human rights, integrating ideas of gender equality into her CEP curriculum. She and her team set about developing a seventh instructional module, one focused explicitly on women's health issues within the context of their legally guaranteed human rights.

During development of the module, Tostan was approached by three local women who advocated that a discussion of female genital cutting should be explicitly included in the module. At first, Melching resisted, concerned that taking on the practice would undermine the trust Tostan had developed with local communities, a trust founded on the organization's deep respect for traditional culture. But the women refused to budge: having been cut themselves and having borne witness to the negative health and sexual consequences on Africa's girls and women, they were convinced that female genital cutting was indeed a human rights issue. Melching relented; she would run the experiment.

In 1996, Melching and her team piloted the new module with several thousand women in four regions of Senegal. The impact was immediate. In the Mandinkan village of Dialacoto in southeastern Senegal, for example, a pregnant woman had been so badly beaten by her husband that she needed to be hospitalized. The incident, which was far from unusual, evoked a response that was: the women of the village organized a march. Leveraging the power of their communal voice and building on what they had learned in Tostan's seventh module, they had secured legal permission to march in protest from the region's governor, invited local journalists to join them, and converged on the town police station, drumming on pots and pans to assert their dignity, their power, and their mission to end violence for every member of the community—women, children, and men. The equilibrium Melching had taken on showed signs that it was beginning to shift, as the women demanded recognition of their own human rights.

The Women of Malicounda Bambara

Then, in 1997, word came that a village in Malicounda Bambara had done the unthinkable. Upon completing the seventh module, the community had decided to end altogether the practice of female genital cutting. Initial exuberance soon gave way to discouragement. Local journalists reported widespread anger at what many Senegalese characterized as the imposition of Western ideals on the village women. The women themselves were portrayed as traitors to their culture. As they spoke to neighboring villages about their decision, the women were met with distrust and resistance. Melching herself was confronted by angry tribal leaders who felt betrayed despite, or perhaps because of, the strong relationships Tostan has cultivated.

Melching called on all she had learned about the structure and norms of Senegalese society. She reached out to her community. Gently and respectfully, Melching urged her longtime adviser Demba Diawara to reconsider his opposition to the women's decision. She asked him to learn on his own terms what he could about female genital cutting by consulting religious leaders, medical doctors, and village women; she urged him to consider Islamic law, what the procedure entailed and, most of all, the experiences of the women themselves.

Descended from Malian royalty, Demba was revered in the region for his fairness and wisdom. He took up the challenge. He met with imams, who confirmed that there was no source in the Koran for the practice and no Muslim religious requirement; he consulted with doctors, who described the practice in all its excruciating detail; and he spoke with women, who shared their stories, revealing the pain they had suffered and the deep reluctance with which they cut their daughters.

Demba came to the conclusion that the elimination of female genital cutting was in the best interest not only of the women of Senegal, but also of their husbands, families, and communities. Demba also recognized that change could not be accomplished one woman, one family, or one village at a time. As he explained to Melching, "A person's family is not their village. The family includes one's entire social network: their relatives in many surrounding villages, in all of the places they marry, even in far-off countries like France and the United States. If you want this work to continue, if you truly want to bring about widespread change, you must understand something: When it comes to important decisions, they must all be involved."[13]

Demba spent four months visiting villages, engaging them in discussions about female genital cutting. At his behest, hundreds of women and men, drawn from thirteen villages, agreed to gather with Melching in the village of Diabougou. Their purpose was to decide what to do about this practice. The villagers debated, their discussions extending to the wee hours of the night. At the end of two long days, the group reached its decision, acknowledging the gravity of its commitment in writing. Demba's niece was chosen to read what the representatives had drafted. Her statement was as follows:

> We, the fifty representatives of more than eight thousand people residing in thirteen villages, declare our firm commitment to end the practice we call "the tradition" in our community, and our firm commitment to spread our knowledge and the spirit of our decision to our respective villages and to other communities still practicing. We would like to take this opportunity to express our deep appreciation to the women of Malicounda Bambara, Nguerigne Bambara and Keur Simbara, who, under difficult circumstances, led the way and indicated the

> path to follow for the government and other communities who are committed to assuring that girl children and women will no longer be subjected to the dangers of cutting. Our meeting here in Diabougou today is the result of the determination of these courageous women. (Translated from Wolof.)[14]

Later that day, journalists, UNICEF staff, and government representatives flooded into the village as word got out about what had transpired. News of the Diabougou declaration spread rapidly, first throughout Senegal and then beyond. More and more villages held their own public declarations. By early 2014, more than sixty-five hundred communities in eight African countries had publicly declared their decision to abandon female genital cutting on their own terms. Tostan's approach has now been integrated into the official strategies of five governments and ten UN agencies.

The seeds of Tostan's success were planted in the earliest days of Melching's time in Africa. Her exposure to the culture of Senegal and to the infrastructure of development saw her toggling back and forth between appreciation and abhorrence—delving deeply into these two worlds while remaining dissatisfied with the current equilibrium. She became an expert in education, building on her existing fluency in languages and her exposure to development models; yet she allowed herself to be an apprentice to the community, learning from community members what they really needed. Experimentation helped her create a community-based model for change and she committed to its dissemination, even as she continued to test how to tackle additional aspects of the unhappy equilibrium.

Yet, as much work as this entailed, learning to understand the world in a new way was only part of the challenge for Melching. Once she had come to understand the unhappy development equilibrium and to understand the forces that held it in place, she had to envision a new equilibrium—a development approach that not only served the people of Africa but was actually driven by them. The change she sought would not be imposed from the outside, but would bubble up from within. The model she and her Senegalese partners built and scaled was premised on this ideal, drawing on all she had learned about the world she sought to shift.

Molly Melching could create a new equilibrium that featured the willing abandonment of female genital cutting only by understanding the existing equilibrium deeply and profoundly. Had she gone down the standard path, trying to convince Senegalese villagers that their practices should be summarily rejected, she would have inevitably failed, as had generations of development actors before her. Counterintuitive as it may seem, it was her negotiation of expertise and apprenticeship—her many years of living within and learning the rules of an equilibrium she questioned—that prepared her to aim for and begin to achieve truly fundamental transformation.

A Foot-Binding Footnote

Political scientist Gerry Mackie, an associate professor of political science at the University of California, San Diego, recalls nearly jumping out of his seat as he read about Tostan. It was June 1998, and he was then a junior research fellow at St. John's College, Oxford. An expert in the study of harmful social practices, including foot binding and female genital cutting, Mackie had come across an article in the *International Herald Tribune* about Tostan's success in securing community commitments to abandon female genital cutting in West Africa.

As he read, he was struck by the extent to which Melching's model mirrored his own thinking. In Mackie's game theory–inspired convention model, he argues that when an equilibrium is sustained by conventions practiced broadly across a society, it will not shift unless a critical mass of people across multiple communities commits to the change. Mackie credits the rapid decline and ultimate cessation of foot binding in China to the establishment of a new set of institutions that established this critical mass and documented a commitment to change. In China, he says, the mechanism for change came about through the emergence of "pledge societies," most founded by that mix of campaigning outsiders and reform-minded insiders we referenced at the outset of this chapter.

Melching's success in Senegal appeared to Mackie to be anchored in the same basic theory—that is, Tostan was establishing a new norm by getting enough people across enough villages to publicly pledge to abandon female genital cutting, which constituted a true critical mass of commitment. He wrote immediately to Melching to compare notes. Melching eagerly replied—unlike, Mackie notes wistfully, the officials at aid and development agencies to which his earlier entreaties had gone unanswered.

Mackie encouraged Melching to spread the word of the Tostan approach. "My wish," writes Mackie, "is that the success of the Malicounda Commitment be understood and replicated now rather than twenty years from now . . . The people who do female genital cutting are honorable, upright, moral people who want the best for [their daughters]. That is why they do female genital cutting and that is why they will decide to stop doing it, once a safe way of stopping it is found." Mackie was convinced that Tostan had discovered that safe way. "Female genital cutting is ending because, after education and deliberation, enough people want it to end," he says.[15] Melching could not agree more.

Successful social entrepreneurs must become deft at managing the paradoxical praxis of change, learning to negotiate opposing states of mind and opposing actions. While the circumstances that pull them to learn more about an existing status quo will vary, their responses will not. They must draw on their hearts and minds, emotions and intellect as they channel mounting abhorrence at conditions of injustice and pursue a dispassionate and appreciative course toward understanding. They must use all of their expertise by embracing the insights their knowledge affords about the current equilibrium, but at the same time recognize the limitations of such expertise and apprentice themselves to those with the deepest knowledge of aspects of the status quo outside their own experience. Finally, they must drive toward decisive action by engaging in a continuous process of experimentation that resolves itself in a commitment, to transform what exists into what can and must be: a far more just and sustainable equilibrium.

Social entrepreneurs begin with a deep, thorough understanding and appreciation of a particular status quo, its roots and the forces that sustain it. With that profound understanding of the existing equilibrium under their belts, social entrepreneurs set themselves up to envision a truly better future and to bring that vision to fruition. The visioning process prepares them to actually bring about the change they seek. But there's more to this next stage than simply imagining a better future. As we have seen in their disciplined and intentional approach to understanding the world, social entrepreneurs tackle the challenge of envisioning the future in a distinctive way, proceeding differently than the rest of us do.

Chapter 4

Envisioning a New Future

To serious motorcycle racers like Andrea and Barry Coleman, flat-track racing is the most primal, authentic, and thrilling form of competition, harkening back to the origins of the sport at the turn of the twentieth century. The track itself is dirt and configured in the classic oval shape. Motorcycles make twenty or so counterclockwise laps during the course of a race, at speeds of over 100 miles an hour. As the bikes roar around the track, they gradually wear a groove where you'd expect to find it—near the center, just hugging the inside. Along the outside, the kicked-up dirt and dust forms what's known as the *cushion*. Throughout the race, riders tend to stay in the groove, avoiding the cushion, where the ride is riskier because the dirt is soft and traction is uncertain.

But sometimes a rider will venture out into the cushion to overtake the competition. Taking to the cushion doesn't require the rider to be a daredevil. It doesn't take unnatural bravado. Rather, it requires the rider to have confidence in his experience and skill, and most of all, in the condition of his motorcycle. The bike must be impeccably maintained—oil, gas, gears, engine—and the rider must know it intimately, down to the depth of the tire treads to the millimeter. Taking to the cushion, with the certainty he's prepared to do so, signals a rider's determination to break out from the pack, to risk failure, and to win.

Social entrepreneurs, Barry Coleman explains, consistently ride in that cushion, where there is plenty of potential to get ahead and just as much to slide out of control.[1] It is a place where guts and determination are required, and where skill and expertise can pay off. Barry should know. He and his wife aren't just race enthusiasts, they are social entrepreneurs: founders of Riders for Health, an organization that manages transportation systems for the delivery of health care in seven countries across sub-Saharan Africa.

For the Colemans and Riders for Health, winning means nothing less than a new health-care delivery equilibrium on a continent that desperately needs one. Today, on virtually every relevant health indicator, Africa lags. Life expectancy is ten years shorter than the rest of the world. Child mortality is double the global average.[2] Whereas the United States has 2.4 doctors for every thousand citizens, sub-Saharan Africa has just 0.2.[3] Across the region, some thirty thousand children under the age of five die every day from diseases that are easily treated or prevented with available vaccines and medicines, including diarrhea, measles, and malaria. Immunization programs, even with the massive scale-up in supply made possible by the multilateral Global Fund to Fight AIDS, Tuberculosis and Malaria ("Global Fund") and a host of NGOs, still fail to reach an estimated twenty-two million children. Progress remains difficult, despite stated commitments to millennium development goals, decades of foreign aid, and billions of dollars in philanthropy. Africa's health equilibrium remains in a stubbornly miserable state.

The current health-care equilibrium in Africa, the Colemans would argue, is kept in place partly by its failing infrastructure. Too often, available medicine and health treatments simply don't reach those who need them. Medicine and equipment can't get where they are most urgently needed. Health workers waste hours each day walking and waiting, rather than delivering care. Communities go weeks and months without meaningful access to health care, even in times of desperate need. All of these problems result from gaps in infrastructure, but it was one gap in particular that tweaked the notice of this pair of motorcycle enthusiasts: African health systems were failing because they lacked the underlying transportation systems needed for reliable health-care delivery.

It isn't the stuff of banner headlines. But in Africa (or, for that matter, anywhere else), if reliable transportation is not part of the health-care delivery system, people die (an outcome Barry Coleman calls, with clear irritation, "pointless").[4] To Andrea and Barry Coleman, the reality that they encountered—a health-care delivery system hobbled by inadequate transportation management infrastructure—was utterly unacceptable. They envision a very different equilibrium, one that marks a step change in the quality of health care on the continent. The future they imagine isn't perfect, but it is transformed in a very specific way: in this future, African health ministries are equipped with reliable, affordable, and effective transportation systems that deliver the health-care services their people need, when, where, and how they need them. And it turns out motorbikes have an important role to play.

Vision and the Social Entrepreneur

Much has rightfully been made of the need for a clear and compelling vision in any endeavor. A vision can set direction, mobilize followers, align activities, and galvanize the will required by an individual or team to accomplish something significant. Vision matters, whether for a business opportunity, a sports championship, or a governmental initiative. Without a compelling image of the future, and—as importantly—clear steps to achieving it, organizations will drift and quite likely fail. Any winning strategy begins with an aspiration that articulates what winning means for an individual, organization, or endeavor.

Social entrepreneurs, too, must articulate their winning aspirations, and do so in the context of transformative change. They must go beyond simply articulating an improvement to the system, even if the improvement is clearly a laudatory one. Social entrepreneurs are driven to get beyond better. The social entrepreneur's vision of winning must speak definitively to the new, transformed societal equilibrium she is prepared to bring about: it must be aimed at equilibrium change rather than at the amelioration of current conditions; it must be specific yet systemic in its approach, targeted at a constituency that cannot effect the change alone while also considering the system holistically; finally, more often than not, it must be adaptable and resilient in the face of changing conditions.

To get to the stage of envisioning a new equilibrium, social entrepreneurs will have developed clear and comprehensive knowledge about the system they seek to transform, as we saw in chapter 3. Crafting a compelling vision of equilibrium change depends on this rich understanding of the existing status quo. A social entrepreneur must be able to assess and understand *what is* in order to see and describe *what could be.*

When it comes to understanding the world, like so many successful social entrepreneurs, Andrea and Barry Coleman saw in the existing system an opportunity that was little noticed by others. Most of the attention in global health is on the eradication or effective treatment of disease. By contrast, the humdrum issue of transportation infrastructure barely registers. Is it because transportation is such a blue-collar basic that it doesn't get much attention? "There's a little bit of snobbery in development," Andrea notes ruefully. Moreover, she says, "People assume the infrastructure is in place. It isn't."[5] The Colemans could see that it wasn't, and they could also see just how vital transportation was to the operation of the whole system. They were able to do so because they had deep and extensive personal expertise that could be brought to bear on a new context. The distinctive knowledge the Colemans brought to bear just happened to be about motorbikes.

Andrea had grown up in a family of motorcyclists, and from an early age wanted nothing more than to become a racer herself. "The day I was sixteen, I put my L-plates on, took three months and then passed my test. I just wanted to be out riding motorcycles,"[6] she recalls. And so she did, sharing a love of racing with her husband, Grand Prix racer Tom Herron. In 1979, Herron died in a racing accident, spurring Andrea to develop a passion for safety every bit as intense as her love of riding. Her second husband, Barry Coleman, traces his own interest in motorcycles to his racing beat for the *Guardian*. It was through this shared interest that the two first met and their relationship began.

Racing also brought them to Africa. Together with their friend, the legendary Grand Prix racer Randy Mamola, the

Colemans had spent years persuading their British racing peers to raise money for Save the Children's African programs. In 1988, Save the Children sent Mamola and Barry to Somalia, to show them how these hard-won funds were being used. The money was clearly being put to good use. Yet what the two men saw in Africa, and what Andrea too saw on a subsequent trip, shocked them: hemorrhaging women being carted in wheelbarrows to the nearest clinic; health workers covering distances of twenty or more miles of tough terrain a day by foot; countless vehicles left to rust by the side of the road or stacked up against buildings, vehicles that would still be operating had they been serviced properly. What good, they asked themselves, was a health-care system without reliable transport? And what good were expensive vehicles that were as mobile as millstones? That, in a nutshell, was the status quo. It became the starting point for the Colemans' vision for what should change.

Transformation, Not Amelioration

At one level, looking to the future and imagining what could be different is an entirely obvious step in the pursuit of social benefit. To make a positive social contribution, every well-intended actor, social entrepreneur or not, needs to imagine a beneficial outcome for her work. Doing so is not an especially difficult task. It's a straightforward matter to conceive of programs that feed hungry children or that provide refuge for victims of domestic violence. These fine outcomes originate in someone's ability to imagine ways to improve life for a disadvantaged segment of the population. But it's worth repeating that, for the social entrepreneur, the task demands more. It is not enough to imagine a way to reduce suffering. The vision must be for systemic change; it must shift the existing equilibrium to a new one. Social entrepreneurs like the Colemans envision a stable and sustainably transformed world that exists at a compelling new equilibrium. It is one that ensures, in particular, an optimal new condition for those disadvantaged by the current state.

The Colemans and Riders for Health are not interested in buying trucks to replace the ones that have broken down. They want to fix the system that lets such vehicles fall into disrepair, and that puts the wrong vehicles in the wrong place for the wrong tasks. For the Colemans, the changed system is vested in the discipline of fleet management. Riders for Health partners with African health ministries, contracting to manage their vehicles, "whether the vehicles are used to mobilize outreach health workers on motorcycles, transport samples and supplies to health centers, or are ambulances for emergency referrals."[7]

In this approach, Riders for Health takes over management of a partner's fleet, providing preventive maintenance and driver training. First, it provides regular scheduled maintenance on health-care delivery vehicles, keeping fleets running over a much longer lifespan, and replacing parts before they wear out to avoid unexpected breakdowns. This maintenance can be carried out on an outreach basis, which means vehicles can be regularly serviced where they are used rather than at a central location—keeping off-road time to a minimum. Second, Riders for Health trains health workers on how to operate their vehicles effectively and to conduct daily maintenance on them, including checks on oil levels, tires, brakes, lights, and other basics. Along with other services, including planning and budgeting for ongoing operating costs like fuel, this Transport Resource Management (TRM) model aims to produce fleets of vehicles that operate with 100 percent reliability at the lowest possible cost for the longest possible time, regardless of tough conditions. It is a model aimed at transforming one specific part of Africa's health-care infrastructure, and in doing so, to make the entire system more effective.

This aspiration—and the model to bring it to life—evolved over time. The same can be said for many social entrepreneurs. A vision of a transformed future may not spring fully formed from their minds. The work of transformation is challenging stuff, and so is the task of envisioning a truly transformed future. That said, the social entrepreneur's aspiration, while distinctive, need not be overwhelming to construct. It is predicated on two essential things:

- A systemic yet focused approach, in which specific constituents are targeted but other system actors are understood and accounted for
- The articulation of a compelling future state—aiming for and sketching out the superior and sustainable new societal equilibrium through which the specified beneficiaries' prior condition, and the system overall, is transformed

Targeted Constituents and the Broader System

First, the social entrepreneur's winning aspiration identifies a specific set of beneficiaries. Like business entrepreneurs, social entrepreneurs' top priority is defining target customers or clients—those who stand to benefit most from the specific offering of the venture. This close focus on the customer animates the social entrepreneur as much as it does the business entrepreneur. Each gets out of bed every day to serve a specific constituency, to change the equilibrium for a defined population. Social entrepreneurs aim to make a difference for someone in particular; for example, they strive to see African girls freed from the dangers of female genital cutting or to enable millions of undocumented Indians to gain access to guaranteed government services.

Those who have the most to gain from a social entrepreneur's efforts are typically those most disadvantaged by the current equilibrium. But determining a primary constituency is not where the social entrepreneur stops. This stakeholder is at the center, but is not the sole concern. In business, a venture rises and falls according to the response of targeted customers, but a company's outcomes are also affected by other actors in the larger ecosystem, including those operating the channels through which it reaches customers, the suppliers from whom it buys inputs, the partners with whom it collaborates, the regulators who dictate the terms of the industry, and the competitors who target the same customers. Any successful business must think holistically about how best to serve the needs of its customers within the context of the larger system. So too must social entrepreneurs be careful to consider their principal constituents in the context of the systems in which they participate.

Molly Melching explicitly considered not just the girls who were subjected to forced genital cutting, but the whole community—the families, elders, and religious leaders who upheld this practice as the norm; she considered the government, health-care workers, and agencies as well in order to build a coalition for change. Simply telling the girls that they did not need to submit to cutting would have been far too narrow an approach. Without considering the other players, it would also have been a lie. Focusing on only one actor without considering the larger network of actors would have doomed Tostan's efforts to failure. Typically, the social entrepreneur's winning aspiration will target its principal clients and make clear the case for serving them. But to be effective, a social entrepreneur's vision must also take into account other essential actors, articulating a new configuration of interests that, ideally, distributes benefits more equitably.

So it was for Riders for Health. At the heart of the organization's work are the African women, men, and children at risk of dying needlessly. The Colemans recognized that to reach this targeted constituency, they had to address another part of the system. They scanned the actors who played pivotal roles in the current equilibrium of health delivery systems—government, health-care workers, and patients—and explored key interactions between them. As they did, they came to see that the health of Africans is dependent in large part on the services of community health workers.

These frontline public health workers are members of the communities they serve, bridging the gap between formal health-care systems and local communities. When equipped with reliable transportation, this workforce is able to deliver its vital services to greater numbers of people over greater distances: testing for illness, providing vaccinations, supervising treatment, monitoring pregnant women, screening for malnutrition, distributing bed-nets, and much more. For these community health workers to do their jobs, and for medicines and supplies to reach rural villages situated hundreds of miles from the nearest town, reliable transportation is essential. Yet development organizations and government agencies traditionally fail to account adequately for it. Vehicle requisition is often part of a project budget or a regional service plan, but the emphasis is on procurement rather than operations. Money is allocated to acquire new vehicles but rarely to properly maintain them.

The result is predictable. In Rwanda, for example, where the Colemans were asked by the Minister of Health to assess its transportation capability, they found its fleet of ambulances showed clear and at times disturbing signs of poor maintenance. Barry Coleman and his team confirmed what the ministry already knew: the reason behind an unacceptable record of breakdowns, with as much as 80 percent of the fleet routinely out of service in rural areas, was poor maintenance. Rwanda is not alone. Riders for Health notes that "the average life of an unmanaged vehicle in the harsh environment of rural Africa is a little over a year. A motorcycle will last eight months."[8]

Addressing the needs of that poor, rural, and ill-served population was a key first step to framing the Colemans' winning aspiration. But for their vision of a new future to take hold, they knew they would have to align the interests of other key actors as well. These would include donors and donor agencies, development organizations, government ministries, and community health workers. They identified a targeted constituency and identified key players in the surrounding ecosystem who would also need to be addressed in order to meaningfully impact the targeted constituency. Envisioning a transformed equilibrium begins with this assessment of actors.

A Compellingly Superior Future State

The second component of envisioning a new equilibrium requires that one imagine and articulate a compellingly superior future state for the targeted constituents—not an incrementally improved one but a demonstrably superior one. This vision will only be credible if it is specific: no vague language alluding to ways in which beneficiaries will be generally "better off"!

What the Colemans imagined was a health-care delivery system equipped to reach the entire population it was meant to serve, a system with the capacity to ensure that even those living in the most remote villages gained access to life-saving vaccines, bed nets, and medicines and to the routine services of trained community health workers. Such comprehensive access would be enabled by a robust and well-maintained transportation infrastructure that would include trucks, ambulances, and, yes, motorbikes. The bikes, obviously, are cheaper to run than four-wheeled vehicles and can cover more challenging terrain. They are also beautifully suited to making community health workers far more mobile and productive, if—and it's a big *if*—they are conscientiously and properly maintained.

There is an old proverb about the way small things can lead to significant failures:

> For want of a nail the shoe was lost;
> For want of a shoe the horse was lost;
> For want of a horse the battle was lost;
> For the failure of battle the kingdom was lost—
> All for the want of a horseshoe nail.

This little rhyme could perfectly serve as a theme for Riders for Health. The Colemans had traced needless loss of life and suffering back to a little-remarked and poorly considered source: the vehicles—together with the lug nuts, oil filters, and routine maintenance—essential to delivering the life-saving supplies and services.

The Colemans didn't start with a grand vision to transform health-care transportation in sub-Saharan Africa. They started smaller, beginning with a project to supply and maintain transportation for health-care workers in Lesotho, in partnership with Save the Children. After six years of hard work, with the stunning record of not one single breakdown for properly equipped and trained workers, the Colemans raised their sights. Armed with evidence that the model could work and determined to make transportation a systemic priority, they began to aim for equilibrium change.

They already knew what incremental, temporary improvement looked like. They knew that when health authorities bought a shiny new vehicle for a region, delivery numbers would spike positively—but only until the vehicle inevitably (and in the rough rural African context, this means relatively quickly) broke down, at which point delivery standards would fall back to their previous unacceptable lows. The Colemans knew they wanted more. So in 1996, they took a big step toward commitment, incorporating Riders for Health as a stand-alone venture and expanding beyond Lesotho.

It has taken time, and has not been without its pitfalls, but the Riders for Health model is shifting the equilibrium of health care delivery in Africa. Gambian community health worker Manyo Gibba used to walk as far as twenty kilometers a day to serve the twenty thousand people in the fourteen villages assigned to her. Under such conditions, she was simply not able to check in with communities regularly, rarely getting to each village more than once a month. Once Riders for Health provided her with a reliable motorcycle, showed how to operate it safely, and trained her to perform routine preventive maintenance, she was able to cover the distances easily, reaching all her patients at least once a week.[9]

This kind of coverage has been the key to improved health outcomes in the regions served by Riders for Health. Diagnoses are made more rapidly, making possible prompt and optimal treatments. Vaccination rates, treatment rates, and bed-net delivery rates have all improved. In Zimbabwe, deaths due to malaria decreased by 21 percent in a district served by Riders for Health, compared with a neighboring district, not served by Riders, which experienced an increase of 44 percent during the same period.[10]

The Colemans had envisioned a changed equilibrium for their ultimate beneficiaries, the rural poor of sub-Saharan Africa. To meet the threshold of equilibrium change, this new state had to have two important outcomes—it had to meet the health-care needs of those it served in a far more optimal way and it had to do so sustainably. Patients and communities clearly gain from regular, reliable visits from their motorbike-equipped community health workers, in contrast to what they'd had previously: intermittent, unpredictable check-ins from weary workers traveling on foot. But just as important is that the change be sustainable. More vehicles, even if more efficient, were not the definitive answer. The Colemans needed to ensure that the vehicles were good for the long term and perfectly reliable. Hence their codified TRM approach. It wasn't enough to tell governments that transportation matters. The Colemans needed a way to communicate a clear and compelling vision of just how transportation could lead to transformative change. They needed to be specific, in terms of approach and methodology.

Adaptability

A vision is not something to be changed lightly. But social entrepreneurs show remarkable versatility in adapting the way they deliver on their visions. They alter their methods, even as the core vision remains unchanged. Again, Riders for Health provides an illustration of this dynamic. By the mid-2000s, the Colemans had succeeded in embedding the Riders for Health model in seven sub-Saharan African countries. Their approach was widely adopted and acclaimed as a best practice in last-mile health-care delivery. But wide adoption wasn't what they were after; rather, they saw complete uptake and universal adherence as the goal—the true measure, in their minds, that a new paradigm for health delivery was in place.

As the pair evaluated their progress, they began to think about changing the model. They had seen dramatic effects from their management of partners' vehicles. What if they went even further? The Gambia, where they'd been active for nearly twenty years, was ripe for experiment. What if they took over the entire transport function from the Ministry of Health under a lease agreement? What if they acquired and maintained a brand-new fleet for the ministry, equipping every health-care worker with transportation and ensuring coverage for the entire country?

With this new approach, which Riders for Health calls Transportation Asset Management (TAM) to distinguish it from the existing TRM program, Riders assumes responsibility for procuring—and owning—the necessary fleet of vehicles, not just maintaining them. Riders for Health then leases the fleet, along with its maintenance services, of course, to the Ministry of Health. Riders calculates its fee on a vehicle-cost-per-kilometer basis, incorporating procurement, financing, operations, and maintenance into the number. Naturally, motorcycles cost significantly less to operate than ambulances, but the fleet structure ensures that the right vehicles are in place for their appropriate purposes. Under this model, health ministries are spared the headaches of acquiring and caring for vehicles.

Dr. Malick Njie, the Gambian Minister of Health, who signed on to the new plan in 2007, realized almost at once just how significant the benefits could be. He recalls that "For the first time in the history of the health sector in the Gambia, we looked at the complete logistics support system . . . I looked at what is best. I realized that using old vehicles would not deliver what we wanted to deliver." Even so, Njie had his work cut out for him in persuading his colleagues in the Ministry of Finance to take up the new approach, with its entirely different cost model. Njie recalls making the case: "Let's put our hands together and put our resources together. We have so many programs that have logistics included in them . . . If we continue the way we are, you don't realize it, but we'll spend more money than we spend now, and we're still not getting anywhere."[11] Business as usual, Njie believed, would lead to siloed thinking rather than transformation: "There are so many Global Fund programs to buy and maintain vehicles.

They come in different forms: the malaria program, the HIV program, all of them thinking in only one direction. They manage their own transport maintenance with private servicers. All think in their own buckets."

Thinking outside these buckets meant joining forces, and implementing TAM in the Gambia. Eight years on, results are very promising. Although the Gambia is a small country, covering some 11,300 square kilometers, its conditions are typical of sub-Saharan Africa. Less than 20 percent of its roads are paved, and 43 percent of its population lives in rural areas that are well off the beaten track. Yet, to date, Riders fleet has covered over twelve million kilometers in the country without a single breakdown. Riders reports not one transport-related failure in referring women in threatening labor to a hospital or clinic. And childhood immunizations in the Gambia are now approaching 100 percent—among the highest in the world.

Reflecting on their journey of more than two decades, the Colemans acknowledge how much remains to be done, even as they look with pride on what they've achieved. "It is quite a long time to do something, twenty-five years—football coaches don't last that long, I've noticed," Barry says, with characteristic irreverence. Andrea is more serious, observing, "I think there is a long way to go, but I am quite optimistic that changes are being made." Both are right. While the change they so clearly envision, a new equilibrium with truly reliable health-care transportation systems across Africa, has not yet taken hold as they feel it should, there are encouraging signs. New memoranda of understanding are in development with both Rwanda and Nigeria. Expansion into Nigeria alone, with its population of over 173 million, would double

Riders' current reach; more importantly, it would bring the kinds of health gains the Gambia has seen to a country whose population is expected to reach 300 million by 2025. Liberia and Sierra Leone, which have been ravaged by the Ebola virus, have also reached out to Riders, signaling a growing recognition of the value health transport plays in health infrastructure.

For social entrepreneurs, the act of envisioning a new future begins with belief in the power of human beings to transform their lives. Effective change agents like the Colemans bring to life what a new equilibrium can mean for those most disadvantaged by the current system. It is this segment of society, held hostage by an unjust status quo, which almost always makes up a social entrepreneur's target constituency. And while the degree to which any population is marginalized, oppressed, or made to suffer will vary, social entrepreneurs will make vivid how the new equilibrium will benefit these constituents and the other key players in the ecosystem. In doing so, they will demonstrate their grasp of all that's entailed in creating sustainable change. For it is the winning aspiration that sets in motion the cascade of choices social entrepreneurs must make in order to deliver on their promise. Precisely how they build models to effect that change is the subject of the next chapter.

Chapter 5

Building a Model for Change

Stretching some four thousand miles across South America, the Amazon River is one of earth's natural wonders. From its source just east of the Pacific Ocean, high in the Peruvian Andes, to where it empties into the Atlantic, the river and its network of tributaries drain into the surrounding landscape, creating an extraordinary rainforest ecosystem believed to be home to more than one-third of the world's species. The Amazon basin is massive, an area the size of the contiguous United States, comprising 40 percent of the entire South American continent across eight countries. But Brazil, which is home to 63 percent of the entire basin, has long set the region's course.

In the 1990s, that course was rushing downhill fast. Huge tracts of the forest were being slashed and burned to make way for cattle and soy, or clear-cut to provide timber for booming construction markets. Throughout the decade, deforestation rates soared: according to the UN Food and Agriculture Organization's Global Forest Resources Assessment report, between 1990 and 2005, Brazil was losing an average of three million hectares of forest, an area roughly the size of

Belgium, each year.[1] "It was," says Adalberto Veríssimo, "the dark age in the Amazon region."[2]

Before the Model

Even as environmentalists like Veríssimo decried the destruction of the largest rainforest on earth and warned of catastrophic global implications, some politicians and economists argued that preserving the rainforest would come at the cost of Brazil's growing economy. Between 1992 and 2005, the country saw its GDP per capita almost double (from just over $2,500 to $4,800) as international trade grew.[3] Increasingly, the battle over the Amazon became a battle of ideologies, pitting conservation against prosperity. It was in grave danger of becoming a lose-lose situation, in which valuable forestlands were given up in exchange for a promise of sustainable jobs that might never materialize.

This put the Brazilian government in an untenable situation, one exacerbated by the fact that much of the deforestation was happening illegally. Due to the massive size of the rainforest, and its relative inaccessibility, by the time the government became aware of illegal activity in a region, it was typically too late to do anything but note the losses. Government was largely powerless to stop the loggers and farmers acting in their own best interests, even in the face of growing global condemnation of deforestation practices. It was an ugly equilibrium, established and maintained by a diverse but definable set of actors:

- Rogue loggers and land speculators who destroyed the forest for their own short-term gain, and did so with impunity

- Ranchers and farmers who wanted to expand their holdings, often simply to replace depleted fields
- Indigenous peoples and rural communities who struggled to survive as the environment on which they depended was altered
- International NGOs, which advocated on behalf of the indigenous people, earning global media attention but little in the way of change on the ground
- Global businesses that sought to meet the growing demand of markets around the world
- Governments at all levels, which were hard-pressed to rein in a situation spiraling out of control

Each of the actors employed its own distinctive model for operating within this context, working to maximize its own outcomes. The dynamic combination of these models produced an equilibrium marked by anger and distrust, the outcome of which was continuing deforestation in the Amazon.

An ecologist and agriculture engineer, Veríssimo could see the effect of those interacting models in the social and economic forces at work in the system. And while he was naturally sympathetic to the NGOs advocating for tribal peoples, the poor, and the environment, he knew that there could be no long-term, sustainable change without engaging business and government. So he founded an organization called Imazon (the Amazon Institute of People and the Environment) to be a "think and do tank" that would engage all stakeholders who were part of the problem to join in finding solutions. To make good on the "do" part of his endeavor, he set to work directly, using one particular mechanism: information transparency. More than anything else, that mechanism was to define and structure Imazon's model for change.

Building a Model for Change

Traditional methods of reporting on illegal activity and enforcing compliance with environmental regulations had proven hopelessly ineffective in a region as large as the Brazilian rainforest. On this front, even the most modern of technology had been of little use: Brazil's space agency (the National Institute for Space Research) had used its satellite imagery to report on rates of deforestation annually since 1988. But it did so only once a year, meaning everything it reported was necessarily retrospective.

The time lag from gathering the data to reporting it meant that the data could only reveal the extent of deforestation; it offered little in the way of a practical device to intervene as the activity was occurring. The space agency's data helped call international attention to the scope of the problem, but didn't provide a way to directly fight the deforestation as it occurred. Faster reporting was needed to enable enforcement in real time. Satellite data presented a promising route, but it would have to be retrieved and made accessible far more quickly in order to give government the information it needed to act. Moreover, it can cost hundreds of millions of dollars to launch a single satellite, an investment totally out of the realm of possibility for a tiny organization like Imazon.

Fortunately, someone outside the system had already made that investment: NASA. In 1999, it had launched the *Terra* satellite, equipped with Moderate Resolution Imaging Spectroradiometer, or MODIS for short, technology. Together with the *Aqua* satellite, launched in 2002, *Terra* views the entire Earth's surface every one to two days, acquiring data designed to monitor the state of Earth's environment and to track ongoing changes in its climate. The MODIS data, which is publicly available, can be used to track changes in the oceans, on land, and in the lower atmosphere.

Carlos Souza Jr., Veríssimo's colleague at Imazon, was a former geologist who'd planned to be an oil explorer but who found himself hooked by the chance to apply his scientific know-how to solving a complex social problem. Using data-fusion techniques, Souza employed NASA's data to closely track what was actually happening in the Amazon rainforest. Imazon began to process and publish data in a matter of weeks, making it meaningfully actionable in the region for the first time.

As it happened, Imazon's timing was propitious. When Luiz Inácio Lula da Silva became Brazil's president in 2003, he pledged to address deforestation. Lula's environmental minister, Marina Silva, got to work immediately, reinforcing Ibama, the country's environmental police, implementing new policies, and turning for help to a number of credible organizations in the field, including Imazon. Using Imazon's data, the national government dialed up the pressure on specific regions, publishing a list of the thirty-six municipalities with the worst records. It also began making good on the forest protection policies it had previously put into place, one of which denied credit from state-owned banks to businesses located in offending municipalities. National and international media picked up the cause, and soon Imazon's data was appearing on the front page of newspapers. Officials at all levels—including Lula and Silva—found themselves on the hot seat, forced to account for their poor records of enforcement, which further reinforced the imperative for change.

Federal prosecutors got to work as well. In the state of Pará, which ranked as one of the worst offenders, a prosecutor traced the supply chain for beef—from supermarket meat counters to processing companies to cattle ranchers—to determine whether products originated in illegally deforested land. Industry got the message: big retailers like Walmart and Carrefour, realizing the magnitude of risk to their market positions and reputations, pledged to stop sourcing meat from newly deforested land.

Almost immediately, the rate of deforestation began to come down; through July 2012, it had dropped by more than 76 percent from 1990 levels, to just under half a million hectares in 2014.[4] The equilibrium that had led to massive deforestation for decades is now shifting—with some volatility—and looks on track to continue doing so sustainably. This transformation was brought about in large part due to Imazon's model for change.

Model Building and the Value Equation

The act of building a powerful model for change is a key differentiator between successful social entrepreneurs and those who have a vision for change but fail to bring it to fruition.

For our purposes, a model is the framework or theory that social entrepreneurs use to shape their work. The model's function is to bridge their visions for a transformed equilibrium to the new state—as such, it serves as the scaffold for getting from undesirable to desirable.

The social entrepreneur faces a steep challenge in building a model to drive equilibrium change. A social entrepreneur can't act as government does and simply mandate change. But neither can a social entrepreneur focus like a for-profit business solely on the customer segment that has the greatest ability to pay. Social entrepreneurs seek to change the equilibrium for a marginalized or disenfranchised segment of society. Typically, that segment has little power to drive political change and limited capacity to pay the cost of an initiative to challenge the equilibrium. It's an ugly irony that those forced to bear the burden of a suboptimal equilibrium are those least able to muster the resources required to shift it. So creativity is required to design a transformative solution, one that addresses the dynamics of cost and value in a new way.

In a value equation, costs are the expenditure of something (like money, resources, or attention) necessary for achievement of a specific outcome. In business, the organization producing a good or service must pay for the inputs associated with its production, marketing, and sale. To provide a social service, government must pay for the time, labor, and resources associated with its delivery.

In both business and government, the costs must be weighed against the projected return to determine whether or not it is worthwhile to expend those resources. In business, the return is determined by the price paid by customers. In turn, this price is determined by the value customers place on that offering—an amount economists refer to as *willingness to pay*. In government, typically, products and services are "paid" through taxes, which means citizens must still see value in the offering to the extent that they are willing to support the government that offers them.

In business, typically the customer makes an individual- or family-level assessment of value—do I (or does my family) derive enough direct value from this offering to justify my purchase of it? Any amount the customer is willing to pay above and beyond what it costs the company to produce the offering translates to profit margin for the business. In massively profitable corporations, like Google or Apple, the value we place on their offerings far exceeds the cost incurred by the company, allowing owners or shareholders to earn remarkable returns on their investments. This is the nature of capitalism.

In a well-functioning society, by contrast, the assessment of value tends to be broader, as benefits accrue more broadly across sectors. Societies are willing to fund police services, firehouses, and a social safety net, even if, as individuals, members never need to avail themselves of them. Citizens accept their obligations to support government because they value living in the kind of society that offers such services—and they recognize that this is in part why government exists: to orchestrate the investments and deliver the benefits that individuals could not achieve by themselves. That said, the assessment of such beneficial social value tends to shift over time and can be very challenging to determine across a society with disparate sets of values. So government tends to focus on products and services that offer value across broad segments of a society, seeking to satisfy the majority of people, the majority of the time.

Government and business both seek a winning value equation, a state in which the value provided by an offering is greater than the costs incurred to produce it. In social entrepreneurship, the same imperative exists: the organization must produce value to society beyond the direct financial cost of providing its services. As with government, the cost is easily quantified, but the value is more challenging because it accrues to a targeted constituency rather than to a customer or to society at large. And while the targeted constituency deeply values the change in equilibrium, typically it possesses neither the resources to pay nor the political capital to sway government to pay on its behalf. So most of the challenges social entrepreneurs are motivated to take on will initially present a losing value equation—where either the cost is too high or the value too low for either government or business to be willing (or able) to pay.

Successful social entrepreneurs, therefore, must build their models for change with both cost and value in mind, challenging assumptions and finding mechanisms that turn a losing value equation into a winning one. Rather than accept the equilibrium and its existing cost and value dynamics as a given, successful social entrepreneurs upend it. They consider value and cost more broadly and systemically, and build models to shift one or the other or both in sustainable ways.

In the case of Imazon, in the prevailing equilibrium, rogue loggers incurred relatively low costs to harvest trees from land they didn't pay to buy or maintain, and the value of that timber was set by markets in which the source of the lumber was an unaccounted-for externality. With no market pressures to behave ethically, loggers had no incentive to change the system. Similarly, ranchers who expanded their operations into land they were legally bound to conserve enjoyed the value of their output while paying only for a fraction of the costs incurred by the overall system. By contrast, the indigenous people and rural communities deeply valued the land, but had no ability to absorb the financial costs associated with changing the system themselves or influence the government to enact and enforce changes on their behalf. The Brazilian government faced competing incentives: it valued economic activity and the prosperity that could come from it, yet it also valued the rainforest itself and the environmental benefits of sustaining it. On the cost side, the direct costs of stopping illegal logging and the degradation of the forest went well beyond what the government could afford to pay. Finally, global customers, far away from the Amazon rainforest, benefited from its cheap timber and beef, little understanding the larger costs that came with them, including the destructive longer-term effects of global warming. The value of the Amazon rainforest to their own lives was abstract next to the affordable products deforestation provided.

This set of incentives sustained rather than challenged the status quo. This existing equilibrium worked well for those who derived benefit and power from it and poorly for those who did not. To produce beneficial equilibrium change, a social entrepreneur needs to find a powerful lever for change, a mechanism that has the capacity to restructure the value equation in favor of the target constituency. There are two fundamental ways social entrepreneurs can influence the value equation to produce positive change: they can cause more value to flow into the system, driving equilibrium change by expanding the value derived without increasing current costs; or they can maintain the existing value produced by the system while lowering the costs. In the best of all worlds, social entrepreneurs reengineer the value equation to do both—driving up value and driving down costs. Imazon provides such an example.

In the existing equilibrium, costs of surveillance of the Amazon rainforests were prohibitive, dependent on enforcement from environmental police expected to regulate a vast, impenetrable territory; as a result, little monitoring and regulation activity was actually practiced, making it a low-risk, inexpensive proposition for loggers and ranchers to engage in illegal activities. With innovative application of repurposed NASA satellite technology, Imazon was able to dramatically reduce the cost of surveillance, while simultaneously increasing the value of that surveillance, making it both broader and more timely. The data Imazon provided enabled the government to take action more effectively and to enforce previously unenforceable laws. Those laws had no meaningful value to the disadvantaged participants in the system when they couldn't be enforced, but major value when they could be. Imazon cleverly employed a change lever—frugally repurposing a technology from another context in a way that also increased the value of the output. This is but one of the mechanisms social entrepreneurs use to build models for change.

Mechanisms of Change

Is there an infinite number of mechanisms for change? Must a social entrepreneur look at the dynamics of a system and design a bespoke intervention to shift those dynamics?

Certainly, context is very powerful. It would be foolhardy to attempt to employ the specific actions of one social entrepreneur in another context, without recognizing the key difference between the two situations. Remember, all successful social entrepreneurs begin with understanding the world.

That said, might there be some common themes—similarities across contexts not in what the successful social entrepreneurs did, but in how they did it? Might there be patterns in the mechanisms for change that aspiring social entrepreneurs could draw on to think through the dynamics of their context and create prototype models for change? This was the set of questions that started our inquiries for this book. To answer them, we turned to the social entrepreneurs we know best: the portfolio of recipients of the Skoll Award for Social Entrepreneurship (SASE).

The Skoll Foundation presents the SASE each year to social entrepreneurs whose organizations demonstrate strong, evidence-based potential to scale their success and drive large-scale equilibrium change. The nearly one hundred awardee organizations in the Skoll portfolio focus their efforts in one or more of six domains: environmental sustainability, education, economic opportunity, health, peace and human rights, and sustainable markets.

Over the years, and more intensively for this book, we have examined the SASE portfolio to identify change levers—specific mechanisms for reworking the value equation that recur across multiple organizations and domains. In doing so, we identified seven recurring change mechanisms, three that operate principally on the value side and four principally on the cost side of the value equation. Some of these mechanisms, it turns out, have an effect on both the cost and value sides of the equation (as is the case with Imazon). Taking simplicity into account, we have documented and classified these mechanisms by focusing on the most significant impact each has on the value equation. Our intention here is not to put forward a comprehensive list of change mechanisms, but to prompt thinking and inform practice. As effective social entrepreneurs continue to generate transformative equilibrium change, we are certain that this list will grow and change. Consider this a starting point.

Value Enhancement Mechanisms

We have observed three change mechanisms that social entrepreneurs use to bring value into the existing equilibrium in a way that drives an equilibrium shift. In each case, the social entrepreneur uses information to create new value. The difference is the source of the value. In the first case, the social entrepreneur creates additional willingness to pay from customers through the introduction of a transparency standard that reframes and increases the value of an offering. In the second, the social entrepreneur enables government action, often increasing government willingness to pay through a measurement rubric that reframes and increases the value of government's investment. In the third, the social entrepreneur creates a methodology that at no greater cost causes a key asset already in hand to generate more value.

Adding Customer Value through a Transparency Standard

UNICEF estimates that 150 million children around the world are engaged in child labor, which represents some 13 percent of children aged four to fourteen in developing countries.[5] Let that sink in for a moment—children as young as four forced to work long days in fields and factories, producing goods for export to the wealthiest countries in the world: children harvesting crops, sewing T-shirts, and weaving rugs. For example, the intricate handwoven rugs that grace polished floors around the world are produced by up to one million "carpet kids" in Afghanistan, India, and Nepal, among other places.

This was the reality confronted by Kailash Satyarthi in 1994. Satyarthi saw a truly unhappy and unfair equilibrium throughout India and South Asia: to produce rugs inexpensively, most business owners relied on child and slave labor, on workers exploited in barbarous conditions. Even as he mounted dangerous missions to rescue workers enslaved by brutal carpet factory operators, Satyarthi understood that such efforts would never achieve the large-scale change he sought. He envisioned a world in which we could "wipe away the blot of human slavery" entirely.[6]

Satyarthi, of course, wasn't alone in his opposition to child labor. But, while most opponents focused on advocacy, working to convince the governments in developing countries to pass ever-stricter regulations against child labor and to pressure companies to investigate their own supply chains, Satyarthi eventually took a different tack. He saw, writes Nina Smith, Executive Director of GoodWeave International, that the children were invisible: "[H]idden behind the closed doors of factories and loom sheds, it would have taken an army to find them. Even if there were troops to round up all these victims, they would only be replaced by more children."[7] To break the cycle, Satyarthi needed to shift the value equation. He believed that if the Western homeowners who so valued the beauty of their woven carpets knew how they were made, they would not find them so beautiful after all.

So he decided to tap the power of the market and bring consumers into the system. He created Rugmark, today known as GoodWeave, a certification system for labeling carpets and rugs made without child labor. If carpet sellers could prove that there were no children at work in their supply chains, they were entitled to put a GoodWeave label on their products. With this new labeling system, Satyarthi placed his bet with consumers, believing their addition to the system could transform its power dynamics.

Customers are clearly critical to establishing any value equation. It is their willingness to pay that sets the price for the offering. Set the price above their willingness to pay, and the offering is doomed. So the rationalization had always been that child and slave labor was largely invisible to consumers, and its function was to keep producers' costs below that willingness-to-pay threshold. But what if consumers were made aware of how their rugs were woven? Could they be convinced to pay more for a product with assurance it was not the product of child or slave labor? If an organization could do that through the thoughtful use of information transparency, it could bring more value into the system and shift the value equation so that higher costs could be sustainably borne.

Over the past twenty years, GoodWeave has seen eleven million carpets with its label sold worldwide and estimates that rates of child labor in South Asia's rug trade have declined by 75 percent.[8] For his tireless work to end child labor, with GoodWeave and in other ways, Satyarthi received the 2014 Nobel Peace Prize (Malala Yousafzai, the Pakistani advocate for female education, shared the prize). Though he and Smith would be quick to acknowledge the equilibrium's transformation is far from complete, GoodWeave has contributed greatly to supplanting an equilibrium dependent on the servitude of children with one free of such unacceptable exploitation.

GoodWeave used information transparency to productively bring new value into an existing system and drive equilibrium change. Before GoodWeave was formed, customers had little understanding of the way their rugs were made, and no real way to know that a less expensive rug might be the product of child labor. Even if a majority of customers in developed countries would have preferred ethically produced rugs and been willing to pay more for them, there was no mechanism for them to express that preference. GoodWeave created that mechanism—establishing two-way transparency that gave rug buyers and retailers insight into how rugs are made, gave a voice to customer preferences, and enabled rug manufacturers who could meet those preferences to extract previously untapped value.

Other social entrepreneurs employ information transparency as a mechanism to introduce new value from customers into systems across a number of domains. The Forest Stewardship Council, for example, certifies that timber products are produced sustainably, harnessing the power of customers to shun products sourced from fragile rainforests. Fair Trade USA certifies commodities (like coffee beans) sourced from small producers who have been paid "fairly" for the crops that make their way to a consumer's table. Though each takes its own route, these organizations all leverage information transparency as a way to engage customers and create new value.

Adding Government Value through a Measurement Rubric

A number of successful social entrepreneurs generate positive equilibrium change by increasing the willingness or ability of the government to invest in a given offering, by reframing the way its value is articulated. This isn't the same as simply encouraging the government to act because it is the right thing to do—these are still social entrepreneurs who take direct action to change an equilibrium. But they do so by bringing government from the sidelines to play a more central role or by changing the role government plays altogether.

Madhav Chavan used this mechanism in support of his efforts to transform education in India. In 1988, Chavan was teaching chemistry at the University of Mumbai (or, as he humbly puts it, "had a reasonably stable chemistry teaching job").[9] Not entirely comfortable with his own privileged existence, and spurred by Prime Minister Rajiv Gandhi's call for a national literacy mission, Chavan began working in the slums of Mumbai, interacting with young people directly to improve reading skills. At the time, Mumbai had a population of roughly ten million people and an adult literacy rate below 50 percent.

For many people working in India at the time, the hypothesis was that low literacy rates were tied to low levels of school attendance. A scientist by inclination and by training, Chavan couldn't reconcile the theory with his own experience in the slums. He consistently observed children heading dutifully to school and saw few on the streets during the day. Something, it dawned on him, was fundamentally wrong. Illiteracy might be driven by something other than failure to enroll in and attend school. He believed it was also a product of woefully poor teaching and an utter lack of government accountability for educational outcomes. He envisioned a new equilibrium—every child in school and learning well. This simple idea would become the mission of Pratham, Chavan's NGO, which aims to transform the quality of education across India.

Chavan started, as most educators do, with the kids. He first set out to prove that India's children were as fit to learn to read as children anywhere in the world, and he sought to quantify his results at each step of the way. First, he designed an experiment: a bridge program for kids who had dropped out of school. The three-month program was designed to prove that "a kid who's eight, ten, eleven, can learn to read reasonably fluently and can learn numeracy" over two hours of dedicated time per day. It turns out they could.

On the basis of this experiment, Chavan raised his sights, launching the Read India campaign in 2007. The effort was designed to reach into both urban and remote rural areas, putting into practice—at scale—a program that could be run by volunteers in all kinds of community settings. At the height of the program, Pratham was reaching 17 percent of Indian children ages three to fourteen and operating in half of the country's thousands of rural villages. Overwhelmingly, the children served by the program became literate—able to read simple sentences and carry out basic arithmetic.

As impressive as the campaign was, it left Chavan dissatisfied. His efforts, though effective, were not enough to transform the education equilibrium in India, in part because they represented a supplemental solution that operated outside the formal education system. For sustainable equilibrium change, Pratham needed to alter the Indian public school system itself. The system was supported by the same actors responsible for public education systems throughout the world: governments, administrators, teachers, parents, and students. As we saw in the introduction, systems like these are all too often locked in a subpar equilibrium, not just in India or Colombia but around the world, for many complex reasons. Chavan zeroed in on one of them.

In his view, federal and state governments were interested in increasing educational attainment. But instead of focusing on delivering effective, high-quality education, they were focused on opening more schools. Teacher training was not considered a priority; as a result, teachers across the system were often ill-prepared and poorly supervised. Classrooms were places children were overseen, rather than places in which they could learn. Students were often promoted through the primary grades without having to demonstrate their ability to read, even at a first-grade level. "No one had figured out the problem with quality. It was not quantified. They could not define it," Chavan says. In order to get the system to embrace an approach to change that leveraged what Pratham had learned through its direct-to-student programs, Chavan needed to shift government's understanding of the nature of the problem. Government, he says, "had to accept that learning outcomes are important." And if outcomes could be quantified, the case for additional, directed investment could be made as well.

Chavan and his team at Pratham could have stepped up their advocacy, or they could have continued to scale up their own work. But Chavan chose to place a different bet. "It's better," he says with conviction, "to go with the government." To change the government's frame of value for the system it funded and oversaw, Chavan elected to design and implement a comprehensive survey of educational progress throughout the country. Pratham's Annual Status of Education Report (ASER) is unlike anything ever undertaken in India. Each year, it mobilizes between 25,000 and 30,000 volunteers from more than 500 partner organizations to gather data on 600,000 children across the country. The survey reaches into India's most rural communities and canvasses its cities. It serves as a valid, comprehensive, and effective means of assessing India's progress on educating its children, gathering data on their schooling status along with their basic reading and arithmetic skills.

The results indicate that India still has a long way to go; overall enrollment is high, with just 3.3 percent of children aged six to fourteen out of school (though, in some regions, rates for girls were considerably higher). But reading and arithmetic scores are troublingly low. The good news is that there is now more than anecdotal evidence of the challenges facing India's school system. ASER has introduced government accountability into the system and been instrumental in helping shift the country's educational equilibrium away from inputs (like the number of schools) to outputs (like literacy levels). In 2012, India's Planning Commission for the first time articulated clear learning outcomes in its Five Year Plan, mandating that they be taken up by all states. The plan defines mastery of basic learning as an explicit objective of primary education and emphasizes the need for regular learning assessment to ensure that goals are being met.

Chavan's progress speaks to equilibrium change under way. The measurement rubric is in place, with the aim of changing the government's approach to funding education and teacher training. Bringing government into the system by transforming its approach to education should, as Chavan sees it, ensure that all Indian children are equipped to thrive in the twenty-first century. That the ASER metric is now being taken up in Pakistan, Kenya, and Tanzania reinforces his resolve and his commitment to sharing this approach more broadly to scale its impact.

Numerous organizations, including Amazon Conservation Team (which builds detailed ethnographic maps to support indigenous land claims), use the creation of measurement rubrics to reframe value for government and bring them more fully into the system to spur transformation.

Adding Value to an Existing Asset through a Powerful Methodology

The third value-enhancing approach is to create an enabling methodology that lets the owner of an existing asset generate meaningfully more value from it and in doing so shift the equilibrium. One Acre Fund is one example of this approach. It enables small-plot farmers to dramatically increase the value of the crops grown annually on their farms in order to escape abject poverty.

Andrew Youn, the founder of One Acre Fund, started out as a management consultant, earning his living advising *Fortune* 500 companies. Then, as many smart young consultants do, he headed off to get his MBA. While he was studying at the Kellogg School of Management, Youn traveled in Africa. There he met and spoke with local farmers about their lives. Through these interactions, Youn came to understand that the value equation facing small-plot farmers in Africa was ultimately a losing one. Most relied on ancient farming techniques and equipment, growing barely enough food to feed their own families—and certainly not enough to sell at market or to lift them out of poverty.

The farmers might have fared better with additional resources and microfinance, as with Yunus' furnituremakers in Bangladesh. The farmers might also have had better outcomes with new seeds and fertilizers, which had the potential to increase their yields, but they had little access to them and without training on how best to utilize these new inputs, results would be suboptimal. So Youn started One Acre Fund to transform the existing farming equilibrium by bringing together an asset-based lending approach, better inputs, and, importantly, an enabling methodology to maximize farm performance.

Youn created a comprehensive, holistic methodology that could be applied by each farmer without a big upfront investment. One Acre Fund, combining training services with packaged inputs including superior seeds, plant stocks, and fertilizer, standardized its methodology to be repeatable at a reasonable cost. When deployed, the One Acre Fund methodology can double the value of a farm's output without increasing the total cost, which enables farmers to earn a much greater return on their investment. This has proven to be transformational in the lives of farmers and their families.

Youn started with just a few pilot families in 2006. Within three years, the organization was serving 12,000 families. As of March 2014, One Acre Fund actively served 180,000 farmer families in Kenya, Rwanda, Burundi, and Tanzania. Within the decade, it expects to serve more than 1.5 million farm families directly, changing their lives by enhancing the value produced by their tiny plots.

The mechanism Youn employed was a methodology—an information-based resource that increases the value of a farmer's plot. This intervention, when deployed at scale, has the potential to transform a farmer's land, income, and life, sustainably. Like a transparency standard and measurement rubric, an enabling methodology created new value by leveraging information that was previously inaccessible, ill understood, or simply nonexistent to create new value. The addition of new value alters the value equation enough to make it viable.

Cost-Diminution Change Mechanisms

Then there is the cost side of the equation, where four different mechanisms can be deployed to shift the equation. This side of the value equation has two major components: operating costs (those that need to be expended each period on an ongoing basis, like production inputs or payroll) and capital costs (those that arise from the one-time expenditure to produce something of multiperiod value, such as an R&D investment to design a new service or the construction of a plant to manufacture products). Social entrepreneurs may create a new model to sustainably lower, or entirely avoid, costs in one or both of these categories.

On the capital costs side, social entrepreneurs can find ways to dramatically reduce or eliminate a prohibitive capital cost, typically by borrowing that asset from others, or can invest in a one-time capital expenditure that lowers ongoing operating costs substantially, making the whole venture more viable over the long term.

Reducing Capital Costs by Borrowing an Enabling Capital Asset

Often, one of the biggest barriers to entering a market or gaining scale once in market is the need to make substantial capital investments. To manufacture products, a company typically needs to build a plant. To innovate, an organization needs to invest in research and development. To enable its programs, government needs to build sustaining infrastructure. And, in an instance where the ability of a targeted constituent group to pay is low, it can be difficult to justify the expense of a big capital investment, even if the constituents could pay enough to cover operating costs once the capital expenditure has been made. Here, the social entrepreneur overcomes this challenge by creatively repurposing capital assets already produced elsewhere and paid for by someone else. This isn't intellectual property theft. It is the old-fashioned business idea of context arbitrage: borrowing a technology from one context for use in another.

An example of how this works comes from the intersection of public health and big pharma. The global pharmaceutical industry is capital-intensive. Bristol-Myers Squibb spent $750 million dollars on the construction of a single production facility in 2009.[10] In 2014, the Tufts Center for the Study of Drug Development estimated that the cost to develop a single new prescription drug was $2.5 billion.[11] This means that pharmaceutical companies face an overpowering incentive to create drugs for patients who can pay and that there is little capacity in the world of public health, outstanding philanthropists notwithstanding, to produce drugs for diseases that impact only the developing world, where potential customers lack the ability to pay enough to compensate for such substantial capital expenditures.

The Institute for OneWorld Health (IOWH), founded by Victoria Hale and Ahvie Herskowitz and now part of the international health organization PATH, took aim at this problem and asked how to eliminate the massive capital cost of traditional, for-profit development so that it could create drugs specifically for the developing world. The answer was to leverage the existing capital assets of global pharmaceutical companies. Through its drug development global program, PATH targets neglected diseases using existing orphaned or off-patent drugs—drugs safe for human use but abandoned before release or no longer under patent protection—and tests them for treatment of diseases in the countries it serves. It leverages these existing drugs, designed to treat the diseases of the developed world, and matches them to diseases endemic in the world's poorer regions, thus eliminating the huge upfront R&D costs of formulating a new drug from scratch.

The initial target for IOWH was visceral leishmaniasis (kala-azar), a fly-borne disease that afflicts up to four hundred thousand people each year in India, Bangladesh, Nepal, Sudan, and Brazil. As the disease progresses, it attacks the immune system; left untreated, it is almost always fatal. The existing treatment for kala-azar cost approximately as much as a poor Indian family earned in a lifetime. The tragic equilibrium was that a person infected with the disease had two choices: bankrupt his family to procure treatment or simply suffer and die.

Paromomycin is an antibiotic developed by Parke-Davis (now Pfizer) in the 1950s and patented in 1975. Through research and clinical trials in India, IOWH demonstrated that paromomycin intramuscular injection (PMIM) offered an effective cure for kala-azar. Because IOWH didn't have to pay any of the costs of development of paromomycin, it was able to offer the cure at a cost of approximately $20 per patient, hundreds of dollars less than previous treatments and low enough to promise true transformation of a miserable equilibrium. The World Health Organization has now added PMIM to its Model List of Essential Medicines.

The elimination of an upfront capital cost enabled IOWH to create a new value equation for the creation of pharmaceuticals for the developing world. Imazon took a similar approach, "borrowing" a capital asset created for one context and using it in another. In Imazon's case, it leveraged NASA's capital expenditure to make tracking real-time deforestation in the rainforest a financially viable activity.

Investing Capital Costs in a Platform That Dramatically Reduces Operating Costs

The challenge of operating costs, particularly in a service-oriented organization, is that they may be *scale-insensitive*—that is, after the initial ramp-up, it costs roughly the same to serve the thousandth person as it does to serve the hundredth. This dynamic can make the ongoing cost of delivering a product or service prohibitive unless an approach is found to reduce those costs sustainably through an upfront capital expenditure. This expenditure is often in the development of a platform for delivery of the offering. In essence, an organization makes a capital investment in order to lower its ongoing operating costs. This same dynamic can be found at play in social entrepreneurship. Some successful social entrepreneurs can alter the value equation they face by creating a scalable platform that dramatically reduces the ongoing cost of a desirable activity. Without the platform, the desirable activity is simply not economically feasible, but with the platform it is.

Kiva is an illustration of this approach. Kiva is a global microfinance organization, a spiritual descendent of Grameen Bank, with a technology-enabled twist. Rather than acting as a bank that loans to solidarity-guarantee groups, Kiva channels funds to microentrepreneurs through crowdsourcing, matching lenders with as little as $25 to loan with small business–builders around the world. Using field partners to vet potential entrepreneurs and local microfinance organizations to distribute and monitor the funds in their relevant geographies, Kiva focuses on providing an online marketplace through which lenders and borrowers can match themselves up.

Before the creation of the Kiva web-based platform, there was no cost-effective way for microlenders in rich countries to connect to microborrowers around the world. Philanthropists and donors could make contributions or provide loan capital to intermediaries, who then identified borrowers and managed the repayment process. What was missing was a means for ordinary people intrigued by the idea of microfinance, and with the means to "invest," to connect with people in the developing world who had ideas for putting small sums of capital to work.

Kiva filled this gap by creating an Internet platform to make the connection for more direct investment in individuals and ideas, enabling this new class of small investor to emerge. These individual investors are now able to find borrowers on the searchable Kiva website and loan them small sums. Although the intermediary microfinance institutions manage the legal practicalities of the actual lending and repayment process, participants on the Kiva platform *feel* directly connected and are provided with a transparent view into the opportunities available.

The Kiva market has surpassed one million borrowers since its inception in 2005 and is on track to facilitate $1 billion in loans over the next few years, all the more impressive when one considers its stunningly high 98.81 percent repayment rate.[12] And it is motivating a real shift in borrowing. Says cofounder Matt Flannery, "My hope is that Kiva could be like a village bank, lending on a massive scale . . . Right now it is in a place where primarily the users are Americans, lending to the people who are in the global south. [But] we are starting to see people in the global south lending in their community, to people in the global south."[13] That is part of the transformation Flannery and Kiva's president, Premal Shah, seek.

Kiva's early adopters and supporters have seen massive leverage from Kiva's upfront investment to conceive of, build, and use this enabling technology. One particularly beneficial feature of this enabling technology is that the original capital investment in creating the platform is amortized as increased usage drives ever more cost-effective results. This means that the underlying value equation continues to improve over time.

Other social entrepreneurs who created an enabling platform include Building Markets (which registers local businesses in post-conflict economies, thereby enabling procurement contracts with outside governments) and Khan Academy (which has created a powerful platform for online education). Tostan, too, built an enabling platform—those sharable teaching modules that could be repeated and rolled out across communities in Senegal, as opposed to leaving each program coordinator to create his or her own pedagogy. The curriculum provided a platform on which facilitators could build rich interaction, discussion and relationships. These enabling platforms drive down operating costs through the application of an upfront capital expenditure. But capital is, as we noted, only half of the cost side of the equation. Leverage can be found on operating costs as well.

Lowering Operating Costs by Substituting Lower-Cost Labor

On the operating-costs side, an organization can take one of two approaches. It can target labor costs, dissipating one of the most significant cost lines for almost any organization. Or it can target its own production, manufacturing, and delivery costs toward a new kind of product or service that is reengineered to meet users' needs at a price they can actually afford.

In many organizations, especially service organizations, labor costs constitute the most significant percentage of operating costs. Several of the organizations we studied took aim directly at labor costs, innovating to lower them dramatically, so as to render their desired outcome financially sustainable. They did so not simply to create more cost-effective business models, but to achieve their larger goals for change.

This is what APOPO founder Bart Weetjens, for example, did when he took on the mission of deactivating landmines. According to the International Campaign to Ban Landmines, "Antipersonnel landmines are explosive devices designed to be detonated by the presence, proximity, or contact of a person. Placed under or on the ground, they can lie dormant for years and even decades until a person or animal triggers their detonating mechanism." Legacies of war, these devices contaminate some sixty countries, and each day, an estimated ten people lose life or limb to an abandoned explosive device.[14] Why so many? Because, Weetjens realized, the greatest hurdle to clearing landmines was the high cost of the prevailing labor. Clearing minefields is a dangerous and expensive proposition. It is estimated that de-mining the African continent will cost $11 billion.[15] Although each mine costs as little as $3 to manufacture, deactivating one carries a cost of between $300 and $1,000.

The job of deactivation is much as you'd imagine. Workers traverse minefields slowly, using tools largely developed during World War II. Dogs are frequently used to sniff out mines on long stretches of road. The job is demanding and requires considerable training—whether the worker is a human or a dog. And of course there is the ever-present danger of being killed or maimed by an accidentally detonated mine. So progress is slow, dangerous, and expensive.

Bart Weetjens envisioned a different future, and created a model to achieve it. As a child in Belgium, he had kept hamsters, rats, and other small rodents as beloved pets. He knew they were smart. Might they, Weetjens wondered, be both trainable enough to sniff out landmines and light enough that they wouldn't detonate the mines? "Some people are thinking of this idea as crazy," he says. "But for me, connecting the dots between rats and mine action was an alignment of the constellations."[16]

Weetjens began to train African pouched rats, rewarding them with food every time they sniffed out explosives. As he told a writer for *Vice* magazine, "Rats are extremely opportunistic. They'll go for anything that delivers them food. And they delight in performing repetitive tasks. They literally work for peanuts."[17]

Weetjens has built a small army of explosive-sniffing rats, one that operates at a fraction of the cost of traditional methods. Nations that could not afford to clear their landmines now can do so, as APOPO's rats de-mine in an hour what would take a human more than fifty hours. By 2015, APOPO's rats had cleared almost fifty thousand landmines and eighteen million square meters of land.[18]

Not content to rest on that success, Weetjens has expanded his rat empire and its repertoire. It turns out that rats can also be trained to sniff out tuberculosis in laboratory samples. APOPO estimates that a trained rat can assess more samples in ten minutes than a laboratory technician can in a full day.[19] But TB detection represents another equilibrium, one still to be transformed. In the meantime, Weetjens's "HeroRATs" are hard at work in minefields across Africa and Asia, beginning to shift the equilibrium for millions of people at risk from unexploded mines across the two continents.

Enabling equilibrium change through dramatically lower labor costs is a key element of the models for change employed by other social entrepreneurs, including Teach for America (which recruits recent college graduates to serve as teachers for two year stints, creating a kind of Peace Corps for public education), Citizen Schools (which uses AmeriCorps members and community volunteers to bridge the opportunity gap by providing after-school programs for low-income students), mothers2mothers (which trains women living with HIV as "mentor mothers" to provide essential health education and psychosocial support to other HIV-positive mothers, focusing on how they can protect their babies from HIV infection), Partners In Health (which leverages community health workers to augment the care provided by doctors and nurses) and Gawad Kalinga (which builds homes and communities in the Philippines through a sophisticated community engagement model). In each case, a thoughtful approach to reducing labor costs proved key to a model for change.

Reducing Operating Costs by Creating a Low-Cost Product or Service

Still another approach to building a model for change is to create a new product or service that dramatically lowers the cost of an activity, so much so that it makes sustainably possible an equilibrium-shifting activity that was previously neither feasible nor sustainable. This is typically not just about stripping out features and benefits to meet a predetermined cost threshold. Rather, it is about redesigning existing products and services with the needs of base-of-the-pyramid or other disenfranchised users in mind.

Since 2004, Debbie Aung Din and Jim Taylor of Proximity Designs have designed products tailored to the needs—and pocketbooks—of the poor, targeting small rural producers who derive their living from working the land. In Myanmar, where Aung Din and Taylor work, small-plot farmers are the country's backbone: over 70 percent of the population depends on agriculture, and most cultivate subsistence plots in rural locations. As the country emerges from decades of dictatorship, the government has neither the financial resources nor the capabilities in place to support small-plot farmers as they struggle to lift themselves out of poverty. Private-sector businesses entering the region are focused on the larger and more sophisticated rice farmers whose output can be aggregated to meet market demands. Donors are typically attracted to easy-to-comprehend health and educational programs that target a broad base of the population, not just smallholders. So rural farmers are left to eke out an existence on their own, effectively denied the information, tools, and training that would decrease their vulnerability and increase their productivity.

Aung Din and Taylor understood this, and were determined to transform this miserable equilibrium. A lean entrepreneurial organization from the outset, Proximity started life as a country office for the well-established agricultural products NGO International Development Enterprises. As it evolved and became an independent entity, Proximity's core task was to figure out how to significantly reduce the cost (and price) of its products. It did so by embracing user-centered design, an approach that puts the customer at the heart of the innovation process. Partnering with Stanford's Institute of Design (d.school), Proximity works to create products and services that are purpose-fit for life in rural Myanmar, specifically designing for extreme affordability. It leverages state-of-the-art technology in the design process, including advanced computer modeling and robotics, to create products that are durable over the long term, but inexpensive to produce and purchase.

In due course, Proximity Designs has added new seed stock, microcredit, and farm advisory support to its line of farming inputs. Those new low-cost products and services have increased market demand, grown the organization's customer base, dramatically increased its revenue, and—most importantly—substantially improved the food security and livelihoods of its customers. Over the past decade, Proximity has provided more than one hundred thousand households with increased income, generated $276 million in revenue, and directly impacted almost a half a million people.[20]

Other social entrepreneurs who adapt and reimagine products and service models into new, low-cost contexts include Fundación Paraguaya, which adapted the Junior Achievement model to Paraguay, and Riders for Health, which as we saw in chapter 4, created a far lower-cost service to maintain health-care transportation systems, at least in part leveraging a lower-cost product as well (motorcycles rather than four-wheeled vehicles).

Multiple Mechanisms

The most powerful form of value equation reengineering is to leverage multiple mechanisms at once, as Jimmy Wales did with Wikipedia, the online free encyclopedia that is now one of the most widely visited websites in the world.

By shifting a familiar, expensive, and cumbersome product, the multibook, periodically issued encyclopedia, from the domain of "hard copy" publishing to the "soft copy" Internet, Wales was able to eliminate significant operating costs related to the production of the books themselves. But Wikipedia also dissipates the labor costs of a paid research, writing, and editorial staff with an entirely volunteer base of contributors, whose work is reviewed by volunteer editorial boards. The venture also borrows a capital asset to bring costs down, exploiting the power of the Internet, whose original R&D costs were borne by the US government and American taxpayers, through open-source methodologies built out and promulgated by legions of techno-idealists.

Thanks to its open-source production technology, Wikipedia can produce an ever-growing and evolving knowledge base that is better (in that it is far broader, more current, and more accessible) than that produced by any traditional encyclopedia, including the fabled *Encyclopedia Britannica*. Over an incredibly short time, Wikipedia completely shifted the equilibrium for accessing information, bringing the power of assembled facts to everyone, including to those who could never afford to purchase a commercial encyclopedia. The benefit to society is enormous. Anyone with access to the Internet can now find largely accurate, timely information about subjects of interest to them in seconds. It also put the old players out of business. After 244 years of print publication, *Encyclopedia Britannica* put out its last physical edition in 2010—its business model had been totally upended by Wales and Wikipedia. Whether Wales can now find enough additional value to make his venture truly sustainable is the next question.

Once successful social entrepreneurs develop a thorough understanding of the status quo and envision a compelling future state, they then must get down to the work of building their equilibrium-shifting models. In this process, we see them use one or more methodologies to re-engineer the existing value equation. Where the original value equation disadvantages a significant segment of society and reinforces power dynamics that discourage attempts to change it, the reengineered value equation utilizes one or more change levers to alter those dynamics. With their models in use, social entrepreneurs are then prepared to scale their solutions, the stage we explore in chapter 6.

Chapter 6

Scaling the Solution

The 2014 Ebola epidemic in Guinea, Sierra Leone, and Liberia is by far the largest outbreak of the disease in recorded history. By March 2015, some 25,000 people had been infected and 10,000 had died. The outbreak garnered remarkable and sensational media coverage around the world, especially as infected aid workers were flown home to be treated in the United States, the United Kingdom, and elsewhere. President Obama appointed an Ebola czar to coordinate the American response to the crisis. Throughout the world, airports began screening for symptoms. Quarantines were imposed. For months, images of health workers in full hazmat suits dominated headlines.

Yet, on a global scale, 10,000 is a modest number. According to the World Health Organization (WHO), influenza epidemics cause up to 5 million cases of severe illness, and between 250,000 and 500,000 deaths each year.[1] The worst influenza epidemic in recorded history—the 1918 Spanish Flu—infected up to one-third of people around the world and killed somewhere between 40 and 100 million people. So what's so scary about Ebola?

For one thing, the 2014 Ebola outbreak has killed between 60 and 70 percent of those infected.[2] By contrast, the Centers for Disease Control estimate a case fatality rate of 2.5 percent for the 1918 flu, and less than 0.1 percent for most strains.[3] And though it spreads much less readily than the airborne influenza virus, Ebola is gruesome as well as incredibly deadly. It takes a special kind of resolve to walk into the middle of this crisis. But that is just what Partners In Health (PIH), and one if its founders, Paul Farmer, did.

Sierra Leone and Liberia, the countries hardest hit by Ebola, are estimated to have fewer than one hundred doctors each. So the ministries of health of both countries knew they needed help as the disease raged. To find this support, they reached out to PIH, understanding that the "challenges of the epidemic lined up with PIH's goals of providing top-notch medical care in poor countries, and of partnering with local health ministries and nongovernmental organizations to build durable health systems."[4]

Founded by Farmer and four of his friends (Ophelia Dahl, Dr. Jim Yong Kim, Todd McCormack, and Thomas J. White) in Haiti in 1987, PIH had "the aim of providing care for the ailments, trivial or catastrophic, that afflicted the poorest, who were doing most of the stupid dying."[5] Farmer had begun to grapple with the problem of "stupid deaths" while visiting Haiti as a medical student. He writes:

> I have seen patients grievously injured, often at the point of death, from a weapon or neglect or a weak health system or carelessness. Some died; those who had rapid access to a well-equipped hospital had a better chance of survival. I convinced myself, at first, that the differences

> in outcome must have been due to worse injuries, greater impact, more blood loss. But with time and broader experience, I was tempted to record the cause of death as "weak health system for poor people," "uninsured," "fell through gaping hole in safety net," or "too poor to survive catastrophic illness."[6]

Partners In Health was built not to supplement existing health-care systems, but to reinvent the economics of health-care delivery around the world, strengthening and building resilience into health-care systems in some of the poorest countries in the world. Beginning in Haiti, and expanding to eleven countries by 2014, PIH has become one of the most influential NGOs in the world of public health by building a model for change that can transform existing health systems.

For Farmer and PIH, the existing global public health equilibrium is as pernicious as it is pervasive. Farmer sees a paradox at its heart. On the one hand, the existing system has driven advances in science and medicine over the last century that have been nothing less than stunning. As Farmer notes, "The human genome is sequenced. Drugs are now designed rather than discovered. Surgical procedures are safer, less invasive. Diseases deemed untreatable as recently as a decade ago are now managed effectively."[7] But on the other, the global and domestic public health systems created to distribute these benefits equitably, ensuring the health of all citizens, have utterly failed to do so. The reason, he argues, is a breach of moral will, which translates directly into the rationalizations normally put forward (for example, that the costs are simply too high to even attempt to address the problem). These explanations, he argues, are a symptom of the commodification of medicine. By what logic, he asks, should those "saddled with the greatest share of disability and disease [be] deemed less worthy objects of care by a medical establishment that privileges ability to pay over need? We are urged to avoid 'wasting' resources on groups of people who are not expected to make significant improvement."[8]

Farmer and his colleagues at PIH see things differently. Their vision is of a world in which the quality of care a person receives is not dependent on the conditions of her birth and the status of her family. Quality health care is expensive, and even with the remarkable work of organizations like Doctors Without Borders, there are simply not enough physicians to go around. Quality health care, then, must be designed without depending entirely, or even primarily, on doctors and nurses. Recognizing that imperative, PIH works to extend the impact of clinicians at far lower cost.

This means PIH does not merely send doctors and nurses to work in developing countries and in response to crises. Rather, it partners to build capacity in local systems largely through the training and support of community health workers. In the PIH model, cost-effective, high-quality health care is "delivered in the most challenging contexts, through an innovative model of care in which local community health workers accompany patients through their treatment, delivering services to patients in their homes, addressing needs for food, housing, and safe water, and empowering community members to take charge of their health."[9]

In its response to the Ebola outbreak, PIH trained and deployed more than 250 US-based doctors, nurses, and other professionals to West Africa. But it also hired more than 600 Ebola survivors as full-time support staff, community health workers, and orphan caregivers. It shipped more than fifty tons of supplies for use in roughly a dozen facilities. It shared the latest protocols in treatment, implemented new clinical techniques, and began to formalize long-term plans with the ministries of health in each country to bolster health care over the long term.[10] As Farmer puts it, "The quality of care in this part of West Africa—not simply for Ebola but for more common ailments and injuries—must be improved." PIH is working to transform the existing equilibrium.

Farmer's goal is to see change of the type PIH has enabled in Haiti, where Zanmi Lasante, PIH's sister organization, operates clinics and hospitals at twelve sites. Zanmi Lasante is the largest nongovernment health-care provider in Haiti, serving an area of 1.3 million people with a staff of 5,400.[11] The organization serves as the backbone of Haiti's health-care system. Its quick work, together with PIH, in the wake of the 2011 earthquake, saved countless lives. When asked by journalists and donors just how many lives PIH has saved in Haiti, Farmer defaults to medical shorthand: TNTC—too numerous to count.

To the concern, then, of whether social entrepreneurs can achieve transformational impact at scale, the answer is an unqualified "yes." But note the framing of the scale question: can they achieve impact at scale? Ultimately, it is this kind of scale that matters, not whether social entrepreneurs can "scale up" their own organizations. Too often, the notion of scaling up leads smart people in social innovation circles to make invidious comparisons between the Googles of the world and all other entrepreneurs, social and otherwise. It's telling that our original article on social entrepreneurship appeared alongside a piece titled "How Nonprofits Get Really Big."[12] In the world of social entrepreneurship, this organization-based understanding of scale dominates all discussions of impact.

Returning, as we have here, to first principles and the primacy of equilibrium change for social entrepreneurs, we continue to believe scale is not determined by an organization's size or budget, but by the change it helps usher in. To us, scale is a question of an organization's effectiveness at transforming a suboptimal societal status quo. This isn't to say that social entrepreneurs shouldn't grow their organizations, expand their base of funding, or invest in talent and capacity to drive their innovative solutions. They should, and they do. But the size of an organization alone is no measure of how good it is at driving change.

Numbers and Meaning

Inevitably, any and all questions of scale demand that we consider numbers, even as we know numbers can only get us so far on the proof-of-change imperative. Andrew Carnegie and his foundation were directly responsible for the construction of more than 2,500 libraries in the United States, Scotland, England, Canada, New Zealand, and even Fiji. Library buildings are easy to count, as are the books that fill them, yet neither number really captures the impact of a library on a community. Circulation data—how many people are checking out how many and which books—tells us a bit more about patterns of use. But still, these numbers don't fully capture the effects of Carnegie's efforts.

We need to assess what really matters: whether a community's citizens are better educated and more informed as a result of their improved access to books and ideas. Common sense tells us they are, and that Carnegie, through his libraries, contributed to meaningfully shifting an unhappy equilibrium. Yet it is important to understand that he didn't do it alone; he was a catalyst, but not the only key actor. According to the US Census data, there are almost seventeen thousand public libraries across America today, and far more were built outside the Carnegie system than within it. Clearly, other players, inspired and emboldened by Carnegie's work, scaled the system more than he could ever have done alone.

The legacy of the Carnegie libraries is a clear manifestation of equilibrium change: a solution that scaled well beyond the initial investment by an individual or organization. What's important here is how that change rippled through the society and how it was secured. As any significant societal change takes hold and starts an equilibrium shift, new actors step in to proliferate and sustain the impact—transferring the innovation to new sectors or geographies or providing enabling support to the catalyzing organization. These other players who enable scale may include customers and the government, but often extend over time to encompass a wide array of partners, adapters, and imitators.

Scale, even when defined explicitly as scale of impact rather than scale of organization, is hard to achieve. It is the stage that marks the true equilibrium shift, and is the stage at which many would-be social entrepreneurs fail. So it is helpful to look at social entrepreneurs who have succeeded in scaling impact, to explore just how they did it.

As with most ambitious pursuits, scale is achieved only as a product of intentional design and hard work. Social entrepreneurs who achieve meaningful scale of impact and real equilibrium change typically take a number of interrelated actions to scale up impact:

- They design explicitly for scale economies.
- They take a systemic approach, leveraging other actors in an ecosystem rather than attempting to work as a solo actor.
- They choose to be open-source in their approach and encourage others to build on their models, either implicitly through context arbitrage or explicitly through an enabling platform.

Designing for Scale Economies

Scale of impact can be enabled by way of a tactic familiar to private-sector enterprise: designing an economic model by which unit costs fall with volume. It is extremely difficult to scale an enterprise, whether for-profit or not-for-profit, if unit costs stay flat or increase with volume. For example, if an aluminum producer starts with a plant built next to a hydroelectric power site that provides it with very low-cost electricity, it will be difficult to grow if the next plant has to be built without the benefit of low-cost power. The new plant will operate at higher cost, and the average unit cost across the whole enterprise will rise. Similarly, in order to double the number of battered women it helps, a counseling center needs twice as many counselors working twice as many hours in twice as much office space. Its unit costs do not improve with scale, and this makes growth challenging.

With economies of scale, on the other hand, unit costs fall as volume increases. When Henry Ford switched from batch processing, in which a group of workers manufactured an entire car one at a time, to the assembly line, in which individual workers worked on a single part of many cars, he created a model in which unit costs fell as volume grew. Similarly, the costs per customer for Facebook fall every time it attracts a new user. How? Facebook has already made a significant capital investment to build its platform. When a new customer signs on, Facebook incurs almost nothing in the way of new costs and can amortize its existing costs across a larger user base.

APOPO offers an example of economies of scale as a route to greater scale of impact. Training a dog to sniff out landmine explosives can cost upward of $40,000, while one of Bart Weetjens's sniffer rats is able to do the job for one-quarter of that price tag. The more rats Weetjens trains, the lower the cost per rat.[13] Through a combination of efficacy and cost-effectiveness, APOPO has attracted major donor investment, providing it with the funds to train more rats and clear more land—which, in turn, has brought its already low unit cost for clearing a square meter of land down from $4.92 to $1.78.

Scaling in a similar vein is One Acre Fund, which bundles inputs—primarily seed and fertilizer—with training to enable smallholder farmers to double their production and income. As One Acre Fund works with more and more farmers, its own costs to acquire inputs and to source capital go down. In 2009, the organization was serving 12,000 families at a cost of $356 per acre under cultivation. Three short years later, it was serving 135,000 families at a cost of $172 per acre. Founder Andrew Youn designed his organization with economies of scale in mind. Organizational scale naturally improves the value equation over time and makes the job of the organization easier and easier. Scale achieved in this way doesn't only make the organization more sustainable; it facilitates its expansion and drives toward fundamental equilibrium change.

A Systemic Approach

As we've seen, the most successful social entrepreneurs take a systemic approach to envisioning equilibrium change and building a model to achieve it. They place their targeted constituency at the heart of their work, but think long and hard about the other players and their stakes in the current system as well. Without taking the broader view, a social entrepreneur cannot understand and overcome likely obstacles to change, especially those that come from players deeply invested in the status quo.

Just as a systemic view is key to envisioning the change and building a model, it is critical to scaling the impact of that model. Inspiring and empowering others—whether the targeted constituency, existing players in the equilibrium, or new actors to the system—is vital to achieving orders-of-magnitude impact. Paul Farmer and PIH explicitly scale their impact through partner organizations; the core work of transformation in a country falls not to PIH but to the boots on the ground, the organizations and government entities that PIH trains, enables, and works alongside in each country. This model produces both global scale and local immersion, exactly the features needed to transform public health systems.

Farmer's determination to shift the very modus operandi of public health—its dominant practices and its institutional infrastructure—has been evident throughout PIH's history. In the late 1990s, the organization encountered an epidemic of multidrug-resistant tuberculosis (MDR-TB) in the shantytowns of northern Lima, Peru. Treating the disease and arresting the epidemic required both the right drugs and the application of the exacting protocol by which they had to be administered. To the WHO, Goliath to PIH's David, dispensing this kind of treatment in impoverished communities was impractical and unaffordable. Refusing to give in, PIH raised the funds and got the medicine on its own. Then, using the community-based treatment model it had developed in Haiti, PIH succeeded in stopping the epidemic.

Partners In Health achieved what others had deemed impossible in partnership with the communities it served; its use of community health workers meant it could make what was seen as an unaffordable and unattainable outcome suddenly viable. In tapping community resources, PIH transcended the limitations of its own organizational structure and assets. In Peru, it achieved an 83 percent cure rate for MDR-TB, one of the highest ever reported, conquering not only a deadly disease but also the skepticism of the global public health community. Based on this proof of impact, the WHO and others such as the US Centers for Disease Control and Prevention have now adopted the PIH model to treat MDR-TB. Armed with evidence of what can and does work, PIH also raised its ambition, devising a plan "to increase the number of MDR-TB patients receiving treatment worldwide from 16,000 in 2006 to 800,000 in 2016." This achievable, large-scale change target has the potential to cut MDR-TB mortality rates in half.[14]

Farmer frequently speaks to the imperative of scaling change by focusing on an ecosystem rather than any single organization's interest:

> Partners In Health has worked for a long time in a number of settings, seeking to make common cause with local partners to establish long-term medical projects that strengthen, rather than weaken, public health. This means strengthening what is termed "the public sector" rather than, say, other nongovernmental organizations like ours or private clinics and hospitals. Against the reigning cult of private initiative, profits, and civil society, we hold that nongovernmental organizations can and should strengthen the faltering public sector. We proceed in this manner because we've learned that the public sector, however weak in these places, is typically the sole guarantor of the right of the poor to health care.[15]

Like Riders for Heath, PIH sees its primary value as partnering with the government to drive scale.

An Open-Source Approach

Whereas some organizations take a systemic approach by partnering to drive scale with their organization as a critical cog, others are far more laissez-faire about their own role in extending impact. They happily watch as other organizations around the world, inspired by proof of concept, adopt and adapt the initial organization's model in new contexts.

The lack of access to capital markets is often singled out as a major impediment to achieving impact at scale. Yet by operating outside the traditional capital markets, with their demands for predictable quarterly earnings, social entrepreneurs are also freed from the constraints that for-profit ventures typically face. Social entrepreneurs don't need to restrict their activities to protect investments on behalf of shareholders who demand a return. They are therefore able to more freely utilize an open-source approach that provides their intellectual property and/or operating model to the world. Social entrepreneurs can allow a broad ecosystem of actors to utilize and adapt their organizations' innovations freely without paying royalties or licensing fees.

Corporations are far more constrained. Google expresses a desire to make the world a better place and supports a number of worthwhile initiatives through its charitable arm, Google.org. The corporation also provides its search services for free to users. However, it doesn't give free access to its precious algorithms, knowing that these are critical to its own ability to produce sustainable shareholder value. Nandan Nilekani had no such constraint at UIDAI. He happily gave away his enrollment platform to as many as thirty thousand partners in order to spur massive scale for the initiative. Moreover, thousands of for-profit partners, such as financial institutions, can use UIDAI's authentication system for free, making the unique identifier more valuable to individuals of all social classes and further encouraging enrollment.

Similarly, Farmer and PIH did not immediately call in the patent attorneys to protect their new community-based treatment model for MDR-TB. Instead, they reached out to the WHO to advocate uptake of their model by organizations around the world, whether associated with PIH or not, in order to drive the scale of adoption required to win the war against TB. And microcredit is a global phenomenon in large part because Muhammad Yunus shared his model with the world rather than protecting it for maximal exploitation by Grameen Bank.

When the driving ambition of social entrepreneurs is to shift an unjust status quo, they are far less concerned with who gets credit for the change than with the change itself. Happily for the world, this attitude and attendant open-source approach clears the way for solutions to spread outside proprietary models.

One particularly effective example of an open-source approach to scale of impact is the creation of an accessible platform. As we saw in chapter 5, platforms can be a powerful way for an organization to reduce operating costs through economies of scale; typically a platform has to be built only once, and then the cost of using it drops with the volume of users. Many platforms dramatically expand the capabilities of the organizations that create them; a robust and powerful Kiva platform, for example, drives the organization's growth, making it an ever more powerful force in microlending and enabling it to extend its impact ever further. But, for some organizations, scale of impact means opening up platforms to anyone and everyone who wants to use it, without payment in return.

The New Teacher Center (NTC) was founded by Ellen Moir in 1998. Moir had been director of teacher education at the University of California at Santa Cruz, training new educators for more than two decades. She was spurred to create the NTC as she watched her bright and enthusiastic student teachers go out into the world, only to promptly leave teaching entirely. "Historically," she says, "new teachers leave. On average, 50 percent of new teachers leave within the first three to five years." The teachers most susceptible to attrition, she saw, were those working in low-income districts and poorly funded schools. That, she understood, meant "the most underserved kids in America keep getting brand-new teachers. We can imagine the effect of being abandoned constantly by teachers on students."[16]

Moir and her organization sought to create a new equilibrium in which rookie teachers were given the support they needed to mature and grow into the profession, and in which children received the highest-quality education possible, regardless of when their teacher had graduated from college. "Novice teachers get no help; they are thrown in there to just sink or swim. I wanted to solve this dilemma," she says. New Teacher Center's approach is "an induction model, a mentoring model," Moir continues, "an approach where we find the best teachers in the system, in the school district, or in a charter network and arrange to have them released full-time to support a group of thirteen to fifteen brand-new teachers. They help them before school starts. They help them throughout the school year." Research in Chicago found that new teachers were nearly twice as likely to say they wanted to remain in their school when they had strong mentoring based on NTC principles.[17]

New Teacher Center grew significantly under Moir. By 2005, it had supported more than 10,000 beginning teachers. But there are an estimated 3 million teachers in America, and approximately 200,000 enter the profession each year. There was clearly more to do than Moir and her team could do alone. So, they created a shared-learning vehicle, an annually conducted Teaching, Empowering, Leading, and Learning

(TELL) Survey of teachers that aggregates and disseminates effective practices in order to meet the support needs of the more than 1 million educators who've entered the field in the past five years. In 2014, through its open-source platform, New Teacher Center has reached more than twenty-five thousand teachers and 1.8 million students—far more than it could reach directly. The TELL platform promises to extend this impact even further. Such is the power of an open-source platform.

Beyond these three core methodologies for maximizing scale of impact (designing for scale economies, partnering systemically, and taking an open-source approach), successful social entrepreneurs proceed with two additional imperatives for scaling impact. These imperatives apply regardless of which route to scale of impact is employed. They are documenting the model and refining it over time.

Documenting the Model

Successful social entrepreneurs typically see the wisdom of documenting their model and its effects. Measurement undergirds most forms of documentation employed by successful social entrepreneurs; they seek to record the problem they see in the world and to chart the impact of their solutions. They also realize that the critical elements of their solutions, principles and practices both, must be fully understood by those within the organization, the organizations' partners, and its funders. Such understanding enables workers and partners who contribute to the organization's work in important ways to replicate its elements faithfully and to abide by its intention. Importantly, it also enables funders to develop the comprehensive and nuanced understanding necessary to invest with confidence that interventions will deliver benefits at scale. Documentation is yet another way to build and support the ecosystem that surrounds the social entrepreneur.

Ann Cotton, founder of the Campaign for Female Education (Camfed) in Africa, is tackling the issue of fundamental educational inequity for girls in sub-Saharan Africa. A long-time educator, Cotton was passionate about educational inclusion. So, in 1991, she visited Zimbabwe to investigate why girls' school enrollment in rural areas was so low. Conventional wisdom suggested that families weren't sending girls to school for cultural reasons. But Cotton discovered that poverty was the real roadblock: families couldn't afford to buy books or pay school fees for all their children. Typically, boys were chosen to attend, because boys had a better chance of getting a paying job after graduation. The families were carefully calculating return on investment and making the best choice they could under the circumstances.

Cotton knew that the returns on the education of girls were bigger than these families could see or feel. Data suggest that if 10 percent more girls attend school, a country's GDP increases by an average of 3 percent. Each extra year of a mother's schooling cuts infant mortality by between 5 and 10 percent.[18] Girls who are educated are more likely to send their own children to school. So a virtuous circle was possible, if Cotton could get things started.

Cotton began raising funds to send girls to school, then founded Camfed to design and implement innovative educational programs in rural Africa. But she realized early on that working with one school and one community at a time was powerful for that community, but insufficient to achieve equilibrium change. To guarantee a community's most vulnerable girls were both protected and provided with educational opportunities, she developed a governance model to ensure the system's accountability to those girls. The model works by vesting both power and responsibility in a set of interdependent, community-based committees.

In order to scale its impact beyond the five sub-Saharan African countries in which it works, Camfed looks to influence the powerful donors, governments, and aid actors whose massive investment in global education is far less effective than it can and should be. Cotton suspected that third-party documentation of the Camfed model could significantly expand the organization's influence. So she reached out to the global law firm Linklaters, inviting it to observe Camfed's model in the field, question its approach, and document its principles in practice. The firm agreed, with partners Lance Croffoot-Suede and Diana Good leading the engagement.

Although they had little familiarity with international development, Croffoot-Suede and Good understood that "the proof of a (governance) model's effectiveness lies in how the principles are applied in practice."[19] Over the course of two years, Linklaters visited fifteen schools across three countries, meeting and interviewing hundreds of public officials, teachers, students, parents, and community and tribal leaders. The process culminated in a 2010 report whose primary title, *Camfed Governance: Accounting to the Girl*, serves to introduce a second title and, with it, the theme of leverage: *Working Towards a Standard for Governance in the International Development Sector.*[20] A comprehensive articulation of Camfed's model—its philosophy, principles, structures, practices—coupled with experiences and hard-won learnings, the report compels its readers to reconsider their own mental models of development and commit to a new paradigm. The documentation of the Camfed model has gained the attention of powerful development organizations and validated its principles and efficacy. In this way, the Camfed model was both bolstered and expanded through its documentation.

Refining the Model over Time

Business models change over time; the ability to adapt to changing circumstances without losing the core of the organization is something that sets the most successful organizations apart from the rest. This is as true in social entrepreneurship as in any field. There is a need to balance adaptation and adherence, not flowing too quickly from one vision to the next, but also not sticking stubbornly to a model that has stopped working.

Sometimes the opportunity to enhance the model is triggered unexpectedly. In 1998, five years after beginning operations in Zimbabwe, Camfed brought together its first group of graduates. During two days of intense discussion, the 350 young women determined that they wanted to find ways to give back, to ensure that more children were afforded the opportunity they'd been given. They also recognized that they could do more as a collective than they could individually. This led the girls to form the CAMA network, a unique, 24,000-member-strong pan-African network of Camfed graduates, active in all five countries where

Camfed operates. Members mentor and counsel students, participate on Camfed School Management Committees, advocate for the interest of girls and women at the community and national levels, and support each other. CAMA also administers and derives benefit from Camfed's business and seed investment programs, thus extending the organization's educational services into the arena of entrepreneurship and livelihood development, well beyond the formal school experience. The adaptation of the Camfed model to embrace its own alumnae and their efforts has further expanded the impact of the organization. But it hews closely to the core equilibrium change Camfed targets—the empowerment and education of African girls.

Similarly, Wendy Kopp has evolved her original model for change in education. When Kopp launched Teach for America, an idea she conceived as her senior thesis at Princeton, she was equipped with an understanding of the current equilibrium, a vision for a better one, and an incipient model for change. Absent from her plan was anything even approaching scale. She had to figure out how to recruit and place her first few generations of young teachers with almost nothing in the way of enabling infrastructure. To her credit, she went on to develop a robust model for recruiting and selecting teachers, onboarding them, deploying them, and evaluating their impact. All of those elements enabled Teach for America to scale its recruitment program successfully across the United States, laying the ground for Kopp to expand her organization's mandate internationally to Teach for All. Today, Kopp's success can be seen in the organization's extraordinary appeal to recent US college graduates: close to fifty thousand young people compete for the organization's eleven thousand available slots. Kopp, meanwhile, has turned her attention from the United States to building community engagement in education in dozens of countries around the world.

Iteration, learning, and more iteration have become a way of life for PIH, too. In fact, the organization suggests that the feedback loops it sets up to link service to research and teaching are fundamental to its work as an agent of change. "The most important thing for a group like Partners In Health," says Farmer, "is not to get stuck in paradigms and models that we mastered years ago, ideas that worked before. You have to keep innovating. The 'learning institution' is not a goofy corporate idea . . . any institution can get stuck. If we are to be a nimble institution, we have to respond to new conditions, whether financial, environmental, epidemiological, or social."[21]

Adapting a model, fluidly evolving according to changes in circumstances while retaining an essential core, is no small feat. It is easy to wind up far from the core values that led the social entrepreneur to start the organization. And it is just as easy to stay so married to a specific model of change that the world passes us by. But for those social entrepreneurs who effectively adapt, scale of impact is possible, especially if they commit to measuring and documenting their work over time. Again, scale isn't about the size or budget of the organization—rather, it is about its impact on the equilibrium it seeks to shift. This impact can happen directly, but it is most often accelerated and solidified through the work of others. This dynamic speaks to the power of a connected world, and to the catalytic way social entrepreneurs do their work.

Chapter 7

A Path Forward

When explorer John Cabot sailed into the waters off of what is now eastern Canada, he and his crew "discovered" what the indigenous Beothuk already knew was there: a sea teeming with fish. On Cabot's return to England, word quickly spread: "They assert that the sea there is swarming with fish, which can be taken not only with the net, but in baskets let down with a stone, so that it sinks in the water." Cabot's son, Sebastian, would later recount finding "so great a quantity of a certain kind of great fish . . . that at times they even stayed the passage of his ships."[1]

Soon, English, Portuguese, Spanish, and French ships were making regular trips to the waters of Newfoundland's Grand Banks. For the next five hundred years, those waters would serve as one of the world's great fishing regions, their abundant supplies of cod defining local economies and spurring a massive global industry.

Millions of tons of fish were extracted from the Banks over the centuries. But by the mid-twentieth century, technological advancements would alter the dynamics there dramatically. In the 1950s, giant super-trawlers, hundreds of feet long and outfitted with sonar, radar, and electronic navigation systems, appeared in response to increasing demands for accessible and cheap fish. The new technology greatly extended the range of area covered, the depth of reach into the sea, and the length of time the ships could stay away from shore, increasing the total possible catch dramatically. At the industry's peak in the mid-1980s, Canadian fishermen were hauling in 266,000 tons of cod each year. Foreign trawlers, fishing just off Canada's two hundred-mile territorial limit, captured hundreds of thousands of tons more.[2] Their combined effect was disastrous, altering one of the planet's great fishing ecosystems and depleting the stocks of fish more quickly than they could be replenished.

By the early 1990s, the once-mighty fish stocks of the Grand Banks had collapsed. Studies indicated that spawning biomass had decreased by at least 75 percent in six cod stocks, by 90 percent in three of the stocks, and by 99 percent in one, northern cod. Cabot's great fish was on the verge of extinction. In 1992, the Canadian government imposed a moratorium on cod fishing on the Grand Banks, marking the most sweeping industrial closure in the country's history. Overnight, as many as forty thousand people lost their jobs in Canada alone. The cod have been slow to replenish themselves. The moratorium, which was meant to last two years, remains in place more than twenty years later.

Before the moratorium, large multinationals like Unilever had been major purchasers of Grand Banks cod—processing the fish into "fish sticks" for dinner tables across America. Now, executives at Unilever were in an uncomfortable position. The near-extinction of North Atlantic cod signaled disruption to the company's supplies of other fish, including staples like haddock and hake. The stark event posed significant risk not only to Unilever's existing markets in North America and Europe but to its rapidly growing markets in Asia as well. So the company took action. In 1996, it announced that it would purchase all its fish from sustainable sources by 2005. Shortly thereafter, it joined up with the World Wildlife Fund (WWF) to form the Marine Stewardship Council (MSC).

The Marine Stewardship Council was modeled after the Forest Stewardship Council, an organization that WWF had helped create in reaction to the threat of global deforestation. The Forest Stewardship Council provided market certification for sustainably sourced timber and wood products, enabling consumers to make informed purchase decisions. The idea behind the certification was to bring consumers into the value equation, using market forces to stop deforestation. Perhaps, Unilever and WWF posited, something similar could work to stop overfishing.

Starting out as a research project within the WWF, by 1999, MSC was an independent organization working to design a methodology for assessing the sustainability of individual fisheries around the world. Attempting to move quickly, it had applied four different methodologies to its first four fisheries, creating a legacy of inconsistency and uncertainty. This fueled criticism from the NGO community, which was suspicious from the outset, worried that nothing good could come from aligning environmental and social interests with business. So MSC foundered, unable to establish legitimacy, develop a business model, or secure funding to grow. By 2004, it had hit the wall; it was forced to lay off one-third of its workers and was down to just eight weeks' worth of funding in the bank.

Enter Rupert Howes. Howes became MSC's CEO at the height of its crisis. He needed to quickly reinvent the organization, building from its initial frameworks to create a solution capable of achieving equilibrium change for the world's oceans. The route he followed moved through each of the four stages described in chapters 3 through 6. To this point in our exploration of the stages of social entrepreneurship, we've featured a particular social entrepreneur to illustrate each stage. Ultimately, though, it's the arc of the entire journey—and the social entrepreneur's progress from one stage to the next—that creates equilibrium change. The story of MSC serves as an illustration of how an organization navigated all four stages in order to effect meaningful, and lasting change.

Step 1: Understanding the World

As we have seen, the process of equilibrium change begins with developing a commitment to understanding a particular status quo, how it came to be, and the forces that hold it in place. The process entails the successful negotiation of three characteristic tensions: abhorrence of the status quo versus an essential appreciation of why it pervades; application of expertise from another context versus willingness to apprentice in the specifics of the particular one; and willingness to experiment with alternative solutions versus knowing when to commit to an answer that can be transformative.

When Howes joined MSC, he brought with him his training as an economist and a strong grounding in the environmental space. A passionate nature lover, he had previously advised businesses and government on sustainability strategies. He was convinced that market-based solutions were needed to change the current equilibrium, which was marked by a perceived trade-off between financial sustainability and environmental sustainability. He brought this perspective and expertise to MSC and applied that lens to rebooting its approach.

His own expertise notwithstanding, he was also able to recognize that he had a lot to learn about the world of fisheries. Soon after becoming CEO, he "got on a plane and went to talk to everybody, went to listen. What's working? What isn't working?" he recalls. "There was a really big period of learning from our stakeholders, who in their heart of hearts wanted to see the program succeed but had some genuine concerns."[3] So Howes listened, and set out to more deeply understand the fundamentally problematic equilibrium in the world of global fisheries. He needed to appreciate it, delving deeply into how it worked, while remaining steadfast in his commitment to change it.

Howes came to see that MSC was facing a classic tragedy of the commons. Each player, acting independently and rationally according to its own self-interest, was behaving contrary to the best interests of the larger community, depleting common resources unsustainably. As Howes explored why consumers bought the way they did, why the trawlers operated the way they did, why big processors like Unilever purchased the way they did, and so on, he found a central cause: information asymmetry. Even if consumers wanted to buy sustainable seafood, they had no way to do it—no way to be sure that what they purchased had been sourced sustainably and no way to reward fisheries that did behave well. In the absence of market forces pushing for sustainable seafood at scale, there was no mechanism to enforce change in the industry.

Both Unilever and WWF had understood that the shadowy supply chain for fish meant that, even in face of potential ecological disaster, little could be done to encourage an individual fishery to adopt more sustainable practices. Fisheries were diverse in size and in their dependence on different fishing methodologies and waters. They were also scattered across the world. Each was more interested in its own survival than in transforming the industry. Only when governments acted to legislate standards and restrictions was global change possible. But individual governments faced a prisoner's dilemma; few were willing to disadvantage their own local industries by imposing higher standards before the rest of the world did so. No one was prepared to move first.

Seeking to understand the world gave Howes not only a healthy respect for the tenacity of the status quo, but also offered him clues to what might spur a new, substantially better equilibrium. Leveraging his outsider status and his own expertise in creating change through market systems, Howes successfully toggled his way to an understanding of the system, which equipped him to spot where it suggested leverage points for change.

Step 2: Envisioning a New Future

In Riders for Health (see chapter 4), we saw that the social entrepreneur must have a clear and defined idea of what he or she seeks to achieve: a future resulting from equilibrium change rather than one that preserves the current state. To serve as a fulcrum for change, the vision must be specific about how the dynamics of the system will change and about who benefits from that change. Creating and articulating such a vision requires the social entrepreneur to take a systemic approach, identifying the primary constituency but also considering players throughout the system more holistically. The vision for a better future must also be adaptable and resilient in the face of markedly changed conditions.

Howes and MSC were not after incremental improvements to fishing practices. They recognized in the collapse of the cod industry a harbinger of worse to come. They understood that modern fishing technologies threatened to wipe out fish stocks globally. The MSC solution did not home in on any single player or variable—say, trawling techniques or the size of dragnets—but sought instead to realign actors throughout the entire system by introducing new incentives and reconfiguring interests.

Early leaders of MSC had envisioned transforming the equilibrium from its current state to one capable of guaranteeing a sustainable supply of fish for generations to come. As Howes engaged with his stakeholders, he too began to envision this future—one in which there was "a virtuous circle of the NGOs raising awareness, MSC helping this to become an end-consumer issue, politicians paying attention to what consumers and voters think: an upward spiral, with companies committing to supply certifiable, sustainable seafood."

Howes's target constituents were consumers, who could enjoy fish for generations to come, and fisheries and workers, who could maintain their income and livelihoods rather than face obsolescence. This is a broad set of target stakeholders, but it is focused on a specific issue: the sustainability of our fish stocks. The compellingly superior future state was one in which market forces drove and reinforced sustainable fishing practices and reinvigorated the oceans' stocks. Howes didn't want to stop commercial fishing; he wanted to create a state in which it could continue to exist without the overfishing it had promoted. The MSC vision was for a global, sustainable, and self-reinforcing system in which certification would drive market choice, and market choice would drive certification. The system that would support that model included fisheries and consumers, but also retailers, independent certifiers, and marine biologists.

Step 3: Building a Model for Change

Designing a sustainable solution to drive equilibrium change requires both creativity and a hard-nosed shrewdness. Recall that the starting point for building a successful model is the value equation. Successful social entrepreneurs must find a mechanism to turn a losing value equation, in which costs are too high or value too low to produce sustainable change, into a winning one, in which the economics support sustainability over the long term. To do so, they can target either the value side of the equation—bringing more value into the current equilibrium—or the cost side—bringing down capital or operating costs.

At MSC, Howes targeted the value side, seizing on the potential to add value from consumers. His particular model leveraged the power of the market by creating a certification system, a form of information transparency. This labeling program could shift behavior across the system. Howes believed that consumers wanted to make good and sustainable choices but had no mechanism to do so. A label on fish products indicating they had been sourced sustainably could change that. "Use of the label in the market empowers consumers to make the best environmental choice," he says. "Consumers are aware of a seafood system. What do I eat? How do I make my mind up? How do we trust these guys? If there's a label, and if there's general awareness, people see that label and it's, like, 'Great! I don't need to worry about it!'" So a certification system for fisheries, in combination with a consumer-facing label, became the core mechanism of the MSC model.

MSC provides a classic example of an economic model whose raison d'être is to produce equilibrium change. Howes and MSC sought to convert the world's fisheries from unsustainable to sustainable. Consider, for a moment, the scope of this ambition. Now imagine the feasibility of building an organization large and powerful enough to convert every fishery in the world to a sustainable model. The massive infusion of resources required beggars description and would be well outside the reach of even a global giant such as Unilever, let alone an organization as tiny as MSC.

So an ingenious cost approach had to be conceived. In this case, the solution was a certification model leveraging the power of information transparency. If MSC could create a certification process that would help drive consumer preference for sustainably sourced fish and assist problem fisheries in making improvements sufficient to earn them MSC certification status, it could create global leverage at a remarkably low cost. The main costs would be borne by the fisheries, who would invest in the largely one-time price of certification, and by the consumers, who would be willing to pay at least a slight premium to contribute to making the world's fisheries more sustainable.

Step 4: Scaling the Solution

As we have argued, scale is not measured by an organization's size or budget but by the effectiveness of that organization at shifting the equilibrium it targets—by the scale of its impact. Scale of impact is often tied to purposeful actions on the part of social entrepreneurs: to design for economies of scale; to take a systemic approach and leverage other actors in the ecosystem to bolster and extend a shift; or to open up their models and methodologies to others, expanding impact by inviting imitation.

Certification standard models such as MSC's are inherently scalable, especially if a platform is created to enable the certification process. Creating a certification scheme is in large part a one-time cost, though incremental investment will be required for adaptation and improvements over time. In essence, the more fisheries that use the scheme, the lower the unit cost of certification will be for each fishery—and the more valuable the certification brand will be. The cost position is helped by MSC's fundamentally networked approach; rather than scaling up the organization to certify fisheries from within, MSC partners with third parties to run its certification program, increasing its impact without adding to its own bulk.

Scale of impact for MSC was not just about expanding the number of fisheries certified directly or the number of boxes branded with MSC's logo. Scale of impact meant fundamentally altering how fisheries operated and how retailers made purchasing decisions so that oceans would be protected. So MSC spent time tweaking the model, especially on the certification front. "The biggest focus of my ten-year tenure," Howes says "has been to really invest in the science, to invest in improving the certification process." The certification and standards had to be just right—not too high to be unachievable, not too low to minimize impact. MSC honed and refined its model to create the balance it sought. As a former auditor, Howes understood that MSC could have no financial interest in the certification process itself, since any whiff of conflict of interest would compromise the organization's reputation and undermine its credibility. Instead, third parties accredited by MSC and contracted directly by companies seeking certification are retained to carry out field evaluations.

Then there were the retailers. While consumers could have little direct influence over fisheries, retailers, who buy from those fisheries, could. Working with retailers, Howes saw, "creates this demand-pull supply chain pressure of the absolutely best kind that brings more fisheries into the program. It creates this self-sustaining momentum that if we can give market advantage to fisheries who prove that they're managing the ocean sustainability, other fisheries say, 'We need to get in there.'" So MSC worked closely with retailers like Sainsbury's and Walmart to get their commitments to purchase sustainable seafood, thereby accelerating the impact of the certification efforts.

The strategy worked. Industry players bought in. More and more fisheries sought certification, the world's largest grocers signed on, new products sought the label, and income from royalty fees skyrocketed. Logo income went from £100 thousand to £8 million in under a decade. Ten years on, MSC has made huge strides, with 10 percent of global ocean fisheries either certified or under assessment and retail giants like Walmart and McDonald's sourcing their entire stock from MSC-certified suppliers. Now 30 percent of developed-world consumers recognize that MSC's "little blue fish tag means it's a good choice."

Howes would be the first to admit, however, that the war is far from won and that the cycle of disruption is still in its early phase. "What we've got is working," he notes, "but it's working best for fisheries in the developed world that have management agencies with the evidence, the data that the certifiers and scientists need. If we are to deliver our vision of healthy, productive marine ecosystems, if seafood supply is to be safeguarded for future generations, then we have to engage in the developing world." How should MSC approach those emerging markets, including those in Africa, where "people don't really look for eco-labels"? And what should it be doing as climate change warms the oceans and fish migration routes change? These are the next challenges, the next target for accelerating the equilibrium shift.

Howes and his colleagues at MSC wound their way through the stages of social entrepreneurship toward a sustainable change in equilibrium, a world in which our oceans would no longer be subject to widespread overfishing. That work has taken place over almost twenty years, and the path has not always been straight. Social entrepreneurs work their way through stages that, while logical in their progression, should not be understood as linear. Nor do the stages comprise a sure path to success. Inevitably, social entrepreneurs will make headway in fits and starts. Organizations may falter at some points, as MSC did. They will sometimes need to revisit a circumstance or iterate on something determined in an earlier stage, in order to move ahead effectively. But, taken together, the stages form a rough roadmap to the path trodden by social entrepreneurs who seek and achieve meaningful, sustainable equilibrium change. Without mindful engagement at each stage, though, equilibrium change will remain elusive.

Where Do We Go from Here?

This book marks a waypoint in our understanding of social entrepreneurship. The work is far from complete, and many questions remain as yet unanswered—some practical, others more theoretical.

On the practical side, how do organizations effectively continue to drive equilibrium change as founders or important early leaders leave? How do successful organizations adapt to such changes? How do their governing boards determine criteria for choosing successors? And how do those successors mark out their own priorities while sustaining the progress already achieved? These are questions that could easily relate to any organization, but in social entrepreneurship in particular, the personal narratives of individual social entrepreneurs are often core to an organization and its values. What happens when these leaders leave the organization?

This isn't a minor issue: of the portfolio of Skoll awardees we studied for this book, some 30 percent have changed leaders or are now undergoing leadership transitions. For some of these transitioning social entrepreneurs, the opportunity to play a role in a larger ecosystem represents a compelling and obvious next step; they feel ready for a new challenge and are confident in turning the organization they created over to their boards, teams, and successors. Other leaders move on to create new organizations, like classic serial entrepreneurs who derive their greatest pleasure from the true start-up phase. And still others seem simply to crave space—to think, consult, write, and reflect. Given the longevity of many of these organizations, we should expect transitions. Still, we wonder whether the transition phase, and this wave of organizational change, warrants closer consideration. We suspect it does.

Also on the practical side, there is room to examine more closely the means and methods social entrepreneurs use to chart their progress toward equilibrium change. We would be the first to admit that this is a daunting challenge. Measuring change in motion does not lend itself readily to randomized control trials or other standard evaluation methods. Often, the most valid measure of an organization's success is complex, qualitative, and closely bound to the work of other partners. For instance, the real test of Imazon's efficacy as an agent of change is measured in the Amazon basin's rate of deforestation, which the government itself reports. ASER serves as a means of assessing India's progress—and Pratham's effectiveness in accelerating real headway—toward educating its children more effectively. How social entrepreneurs develop feedback loops with their targeted beneficiaries is a particularly promising line of inquiry here.

In terms of theory, to what extent is "innovation" truly at the heart of social entrepreneurship, as many of us have assumed? In looking at the mechanisms social entrepreneurs deploy to build their models—at the role, for example, of repurposing an existing technology or shifting a proven approach from one context to another—it is clear that invention is not always part of an intervention. Indeed, many of the strongest and most successful social entrepreneurs have dedicated their efforts not to "new" ideas but to the hard and slogging work of infrastructure building. As Paul Farmer recounts, when he was first called a social entrepreneur, he was puzzled. "What, exactly, is a social entrepreneur?" he recalls wondering. "I know I'm a doctor and an anthropologist, but part of me winced as I acknowledged that, yes, we live in an era in which simply seeking to provide high-quality medical care to the world's poorest is considered innovative and entrepreneurial. Thus the diagnosis comes with both honor and shame. Shouldn't we have long ago offered such services to those who need them most? Shouldn't we have designed systems to solve the health problems faced by the world's bottom billion?"[4]

Also on the theoretical side, to what extent do social entrepreneurs share common mind-sets or personal characteristics that could be helpful to understanding and extending the phenomenon of social entrepreneurship? As we seek to understand how social entrepreneurs do what they do, it is quite common to imbue them with a set of attributes. We did so ourselves, in "Social Entrepreneurship: The Case for Definition."[5] There, we identified creativity, courage, and fortitude as qualities we felt were characteristic of social entrepreneurs. In an early draft of this book, we tweaked our terminology to creativity, perseverance, and faith. But are these qualities indeed distinctive to social entrepreneurs, or are they more broadly relevant to leaders across all domains?

To what extent are women and men engaged in the disciplined pursuit of societal change a breed apart when it comes to their leadership? This too is a question worthy of further examination.

As we explored the question of core attributes, we concluded that it is important not to deify social entrepreneurs. Many are indeed exceptional human beings driven to make change where others either give up or despair, and we do think of them as "uncommon heroes"—the antithesis to many of the sports stars and celebrities lionized in popular culture. But they are also people—women and men who hit walls in their personal and professional lives, who struggle to balance their commitments, who have egos, failings, and bad days. It is therefore important to temper our instinct to paint them as bigger than life. They aren't. Their ambitions and dreams are not unlike those of any thoughtful person. They want for the world and humanity what most of us want: more equitable societies, healthier people, clean air, a sustainable environment, and the chance for our fellow human beings to develop their gifts. The difference is their willingness to take direct action to achieve such outcomes.

As inquiry continues into this still nascent field, we are hopeful that the on-the-ground practice of social entrepreneurship, the experience of social entrepreneurs, will continue to inform it. We hope that ever more people will strive to change unjust equilibriums in the world, leveraging the mechanisms for change we have explored and inventing new ones. And we hope that as the field continues to become more established and readily understood, more funders will dedicate resources to helping social entrepreneurs build their transformational models. Finally, we hope that actors in the domains of government and business will adopt and adapt the tools of social entrepreneurship to accelerate their own work.

Equilibrium Change

Equilibrium change isn't a new concept. But traditionally, it has been achieved through one of two means: government-led innovation and business-led innovation. Increasingly, though, as this book has shown, there is a growing appreciation for how social change can arise and be advanced from the space between the two institutional domains. Expanding ranks of highly motivated innovators see this as-yet unclaimed space as fertile ground for improving the world. Operating outside the strict purview of government or business, while remaining mindful of their advantages and limitations, social entrepreneurs operating in this space are uniquely able to borrow and adapt from both in their pursuit of equilibrium change.

For social entrepreneurs, simply making things better isn't good enough. They imagine the future as it should be, and they ask "Why not?" Then they get to work, determined with every stride forward, with every inevitable setback, to go beyond better. Yet no individual—no matter how brilliant and driven—can effect societal change without partners, a supportive system, and most important of all, solidarity with those ill-served by the current status quo. Again and again, social entrepreneurs put their faith in those whose lot in life has been determined not by destiny but by an unjust status quo. It is belief in the capacity of Senegal's women and men that drives Molly Melching in her work with Tostan. Paul

Farmer is unequivocal on the excellence of the community-based care model Partners In Health has practiced over thirty years: "Whether we have lots of doctors, or very few, community-based care is the highest standard of care for chronic disease." And Vicky Colbert knows, without doubt, that every educational system, no matter where it's based or how resource-constrained, can be transformed into an optimal learning experience for children and their teachers.

Within every social entrepreneur is a belief that even the most intractable problem offers an opportunity for change. Instead of cursing the darkness, social entrepreneurs shine a light on what might be different. They confront the societal structures that leave too many behind, roll up their sleeves, and set about the hard, exhilarating, and important work of transforming what is into what can and should be.

With the drivers of change—and a four-stage model for achieving it—better understood, our hope is that more social entrepreneurs will find their way forward more quickly and effectively, with more funders and supporters stepping up to help them achieve sustainable change. As more social entrepreneurs succeed in transforming injustice and righting the world, we all stand to benefit. Yes, the world can get beyond better—and social entrepreneurs prove it's possible.

Notes

Introduction

1. Andrew Carnegie, *The Autobiography of Andrew Carnegie* (London: Constable & Co, 1920).

2. Ibid., 28.

3. *Wikipedia*, s.v. "Carnegie Library," last modified May 4, 2015, http://en.wikipedia.org/wiki/Carnegie_library.

4. Donald A. Schön, *The Reflective Practitioner: How Professionals Think in Action* (New York: Basic Books, 1983).

5. Roger L. Martin and Sally Osberg. "Social Entrepreneurship: The Case for Definition." *Stanford Social Innovation Review* 5, no. 2 (Spring 2007): 28–39.

6. Cited in Danielle Kurtzleben, "Income Gap Between Young College and High School Grads Widens." *U.S. News and World Report*, February 11, 2014.

7. E. Mark Hanson, *Educational Reform and Administration Development: The Cases of Colombia and Venezuela* (Palo Alto, CA: Hoover Press Publication, 1986).

8. All quotes from Vicky Colbert are taken from an interview with Jennifer Riel, conducted on April 8, 2013.

9. David L. Kirp, "Make School a Democracy," *New York Times Sunday Review*, March 1, 2015.

10. Ashoka, *2012 Annual Report*. https://www.ashoka.org/files/Ashoka-Annual-Report-FY12.pdf.

Chapter 1

1. Thomas S. Kuhn, *The Structure of Scientific Revolutions* (Chicago: University of Chicago Press, 1962).

2. David Sheff, "Playboy Interview: Steve Jobs" *Playboy*, February 1985.

Chapter 2

1. Muhammad Yunus, *Banker to the Poor: Micro-Lending and the Battle Against World Poverty* (New York: PublicAffairs, 1999).
2. "Face Value: Macro Credit." *The Economist*, October 19, 2006.
3. Muhammad Yunus, "Eliminating Poverty through Market-Based Social Entrepreneurship," *Global Urban Development Magazine*, May 2005.
4. Grameen Bank home page, http://www.grameen-info.org/index.php?option=com_content&task=view&id=26&Itemid=165.
5. "The Nobel Peace Prize 2006," http://www.nobelprize.org/nobel_prizes/peace/laureates/2006/.
6. Unless otherwise noted, all quotes from Sir Ronald Cohen are taken from an interview for this book with Jennifer Riel, conducted on May 12, 2014.
7. Daniel Pink, "Why the World Is Flat," *Wired*, May 2005.
8. Nandan Nilekani, *Imagining India: The Idea of a Renewed Nation* (London: Penguin, 2008).
9. All quotes from Nandan Nilekani are taken from an interview with Roger Martin and Jennifer Riel, conducted on May 21, 2014.
10. "Economic Survey 2015: JAM Number trinity to help offer support to poor households," Economictimes.com, http://economictimes.indiatimes.com/news/economy/policy/economic-survey-2015-jam-number-trinity-to-help-offer-support-to-poor-households/articleshow/46394256.cms.
11. Surabhi Agarwal, "Aadhaar: UPA-II's Pet Project Faces Rough Weather," *Business Standard*, April 4, 2014.

Chapter 3

1. Dorothy Ko, *Cinderella's Sisters: A Revisionist History of Footbinding* (Berkeley, CA: University of California Press, 2005), 9.

2. Amanda Foreman, "Why Footbinding Persisted in China for a Millennium," *Smithsonian Magazine,* February 2015, http://www.smithsonianmag.com/history/why-footbinding-persisted-china-millennium-180953971/#Z83e5q6hlOvyd pSh.99.

3. Kwame Anthony Appiah, "The Art of Social Change," *New York Times*, October 22, 2010, http://www.nytimes.com/2010/10/24/magazine/24FOB-Footbinding-t.html?pagewanted=all&_r=0.

4. Aimee Molloy, *However Long the Night: Molly Melching's Journey to Help Millions of African Women and Girls Triumph* (New York: HarperOne, 2013), 37. Unless otherwise noted, all Molly Melching quotes are taken from this book.

5. Interview with Skoll Foundation, conducted on April 2013.

6. Molloy, *However Long the Night,* 56.

7. Dennis Whittle, *How Feedback Loops Can Improve Aid (and Maybe Governance)*, Center for Global Development, August 13, 2013, http://www.cgdev.org/publication/how-feedback-loops-can-improve-aid-and-maybe-governance.

8. Interview with Jennifer Riel, conducted on April 2013.

9. Molloy, *However Long the Night*, 59.

10. World Health Organization, *Female Genital Mutilation*, February 2014, http://www.who.int/mediacentre/factsheets/fs241/en/.

11. Molloy, *However Long the Night*, 114.

12. Ibid., 117.

13. Gannon Gillespie, "Ending Female Genital Mutilation, One Household at a Time," *The Guardian*, August 22, 2013.

14. "February 14, 1998: The First Inter-Village Public Declaration." *Tostan Blog*, February 14, 2015, http://www.tostan.org/blog/february-14-1998-first-inter-village-public-declaration.

15. Gerry Mackie, "A Way to End Female Genital Cutting," The Female Genital Cutting Education and Networking Project, http://www.fgmnetwork.org/articles/mackie1998.php.

Chapter 4

1. Conversation between Barry Coleman and Sally Osberg, conducted on July 20, 2010.

2. "The State of Healthcare in Africa." KPMG Africa.com, 2012, http://www.kpmg.com/Africa/en/IssuesAndInsights/Articles-Publications/Documents/The-State-of-Healthcare-in-Africa.pdf.

3. World Bank, "Physicians (per 1,000 people), 2010, http://data.worldbank.org/indicator/SH.MED.PHYS.ZS?order=wbapi_data_value_2010+wbapi_data_value+wbapi_data_value-first&sort=asc.

4. Unless otherwise noted, all quotes from Barry and Andrea Coleman are taken from an interview with Jennifer Riel, conducted on April 10, 2013.

5. Kerry A. Dolan, "The Surprising Link Between Motorcycles and Better African Health Care," *Forbes.com*, October 25, 2012.

6. Serena Tarling, "Why Healthcare Workers in Africa Are Being Turned into Bikers," *Financial Times*, December 13, 2013.

7. Riders for Health, "Fleet Management," 2012, http://www.riders.org/what-we-do/our-services/fleet-management.

8. Riders for Health, *Annual Report and Accounts, 2004*, https://riders-live-cms.s3.amazonaws.com/AnualReports/2004.pdf.

9. Hau L. Lee, Sonali V. Rammohan, and Lesley Sept, "Innovative Logistics in Extreme Conditions: Lessons from Gambia," *Supply Chain Management Review*, November 2011.

10. Riders for Health, "Training Is Key to Mobilising Health Workers," August, 28, 2008, http://www.riders.org/news-blog/news/training-is-key-to-mobilising-health-workers.

11. Sonali Rammohan, Riders for Health—*A Fleet Leasing Model in the Gambia*, case study, Riders for Health, April 2010, https://riders-live-cms.s3.amazonaws.com/Research/A%20Fleet%20Leasing%20Model%20in%20the%20Gambia%20-%20Stanford%20University%20Case%20Study.pdf.

Chapter 5

1. Food and Agriculture Organization of the United Nations, "Global Forest Resources Assessment 2010," http://www.fao.org/forestry/fra/fra2010/en/.

2. All quotes from Adalberto Veríssimo are from a Skoll Foundation interview with Michael Schwartz, conducted on December 2011.

3. World Bank, "GDP Per Capita," http://data.worldbank.org/indicator/NY.GDP.PCAP.CD?page=1.

4. "Deforestation Down 27 Percent Since 2011," *Daily Express*, November 27, 2012, http://www.express.co.uk/news/world/361048/Deforestation-down-27-since-2011; Ministério de Ciência e Tecnologia, "Annual Rates of Deforestation," http://www.obt.inpe.br/prodes/prodes_1988_2014.htm.

5. UNICEF, *Child Labor: Current Status and Progress*, http://data.unicef.org/child-protection/child-labor.

6. "Profile: Kailash Satyarthi," *BBC News*, December 10, 2014, http://www.bbc.com/news/world-asia-29568634.

7. Nina Smith, "Nobel Prize Winner Kailash Satyarthi: An Engineer of Freedom," *Christian Science Monitor*, October 21, 2014, http://www.csmonitor.com/World/Making-a-difference/Change-Agent/2014/1021/Nobel-Prize-winner-Kailash-Satyarthi-an-engineer-of-freedom.

8. GoodWeave, "How to Become a GoodWeave Industry Supporter," http://www.goodweave.org.uk/our-retailers/how-to-become-a-retail-partner.shtml.

9. Unless otherwise noted, all Madhav Chavan quotes are from an interview with Jennifer Riel and Cindy Chen, conducted on April 5, 2014.

10. Patricia Van Arnum, "Evaluating Big Pharma's Manufacturing Investment Plans," *PharmaExec.com*, September 9, 2013. http://www.pharmexec.com/evaluating-big-pharmas-manufacturing-investment-plans.

11. Rick Mullin and *Chemical & Engineering News*, "Cost to Develop New Pharmaceutical Drug Now Exceeds $2.5B," *Scientific American*, November 24, 2014, http://www.scientificamerican.com/article/cost-to-develop-new-pharmaceutical-drug-now-exceeds-2-5b/.

12. Kiva, "About Us," http://www.kiva.org/about.

13. Quote is from an interview with Jennifer Riel, conducted on April 9, 2013.

14. International Campaign to Ban Landmines, "Why Landmines Are Still a Problem," http://www.icbl.org/en-gb/problem/why-landmines-are-still-a-problem.aspx.

15. Rebecca Burn-Callander, "Meet the British Company Clearing Up the Minefields of the World," *The Telegraph*, November 15, 2014. http://www.telegraph.co.uk/finance/businessclub/sales/11232365/Meet-the-British-company-clearing-up-the-minefields-of-the-world.html.

16. James Rippingale, "An Army of Giant African Pouched Rats Are Clearing Mozambique's Minefields," *Vice*, September 17, 2014, http://www.vice.com/read/this-ngo-trains-giant-rats-to-clear-minefields-182.

17. Ibid.

18. APOPO, "Our Results: Impact," https://www.apopo.org/en/about/results/impact.

19. APOPO, "Tuberculosis Detection," https://www.apopo.org/en/tuberculosis-detection/projects.

20. Proximity Designs, "Our Work in Numbers," http://www.proximitydesigns.org/impact/numbers.

Chapter 6

1. James Simpson, "Ebola Pandemic: Risks and Realities," *Accuracy in Media,* October 22, 2014, http://www.aim.org/special-report/ebola-pandemic-risks-and-realities/.

2. James Gallagher, "Ebola: How Does It Compare?" *BBC*, December 28, 2014, http://www.bbc.com/news/health-29953765.

3. Jeffery K. Taubenberger and David M. Morens, "1918 Influenza: The Mother of All Pandemics," *Emerging Infectious Diseases* 12, no. 1 (January 2006), http://wwwnc.cdc.gov/eid/article/12/1/05-0979_article.

4. Partners In Health, "Ebola," http://www.pih.org/blog/partners-in-health-ebola-response.

5. Paul Farmer, "Who Lives and Who Dies: Who Survives?" *London Review of Books*, February 5, 2015, http://www.lrb.co.uk/v37/n03/paul-farmer/who-lives-and-who-dies.

6. Ibid.

7. Paul Farmer, *To Repair the World: Paul Farmer Speaks to the Next Generation,* Jonathan Weigel, ed. (Berkeley and Los Angeles, CA: University of California Press, 2013), 16.

8. Ibid., 4.

9. Skoll Foundation, "Partners In Health," http://www.skollfoundation.org/entrepreneur/dr-paul-farmer/.

10. Partners In Health, "Ebola."

11. Partners In Health, "Haiti," http://www.pih.org/country/haiti/about.

12. William Foster and Gail Fine, "How Nonprofits Get Really Big," *Stanford Social Innovation Review* 14 (Spring 2007), http://www.ssireview.org/articles/entry/how_nonprofits_get_really_big.

13. Matthew M. Burke, "Rats May Be Cheaper Alternative to IED-Seeking Dogs," *Stars and Stripes*, August 25, 2012, http://www.stripes.com/news/rats-may-be-cheaper-alternative-to-ied-seeking-dogs-1.186930.

14. Partners In Health, "Tuberculosis," https://owa.pih.org/issues/tb.html.

15. Haun Saussy, ed., *Partner to the Poor: A Paul Farmer Reader* (Berkeley: University of California Press, 2010), 495.

16. All quotes from Ellen Moir are taken from an interview with Jennifer Riel, conducted on April 7, 2013.

17. New Teacher Center, "Retention," http://www.newteacher-center.org/impact/retention.

18. Plan International Canada, Inc., "Girls' Education," http://becauseiamagirl.ca/girlseducation.

19. Acevo, "Governance," https://www.acevo.org.uk/advice-support/governance.

20. Linklaters, *Camfed Governance: Accounting to the Girl: Working Towards a Standard for Governance in the International Development Sector*, April 2010, https://camfed.org/media/uploads/files/Camfed_Linklaters_Accounting_to_the_Girl.pdf.

21. Saussy, *Partner to the Poor*, 574.

Chapter 7

1. Callum Roberts, *The Unnatural History of the Sea* (Washington, DC: Island Press, 2007), 33.

2. Janet Thomson and Manmeet Ahluwalia, "Remembering the Mighty Cod Fishery 20 Years After Moratorium," *CBCNews*, June 29, 2012, http://www.cbc.ca/news/canada/remembering-the-mighty-cod-fishery-20-years-after-moratorium-1.1214172.

3. Unless otherwise noted, all Rupert Howes quotes come from an interview with Jennifer Riel, conducted on April 11, 2013.

4. Paul Farmer, *To Repair the World: Paul Farmer Speaks to the Next Generation,* Jonathan Weigel, ed. (Berkeley and Los Angeles, CA: University of California Press, 2013), 32–33.

5. Roger L. Martin and Sally Osberg, "Social Entrepreneurship: The Case for Definition," *Stanford Social Innovation Review* 5, no. 2 (Spring 2007): 28–39.

Bibliography

Social Entrepreneurship: Introducing the Concept and How It Works

Alvord, Sarah H., L. David Brown, and Christine W. Letts. "Social Entrepreneurship and Social Transformation: An Exploratory Study." Working Paper No. 15. Hauser Center for Nonprofit Organizations, Harvard Kennedy School, Cambridge, MA, November 2002.

Austin, James, Howard Stevenson, and Jane Wei-Skillern. "Social and Commercial Entrepreneurship: Same, Different, or Both?" *Entrepreneurship Theory and Practice* 30, no. 1 (2006): 1–22.

Bloom, Paul N., and J. Gregory Dees. "Cultivate Your Ecosystem." *Stanford Social Innovation Review* 6, no. 1 (Winter 2008): 47–53.

Bornstein, David, and Susan Davis. *Social Entrepreneurship: What Everyone Needs to Know.* New York: Oxford University Press, 2010.

Dees, J. Gregory. "The Meaning of 'Social Entrepreneurship.'" Center for Social Innovation, Stanford School of Business, October 31, 1998; (rev.) May 30, 2001. http://csi.gsb.stanford.edu/the-meaning-social-entrepreneurship.

Dees, J. Gregory. "A Tale of Two Cultures: Charity, Problem Solving, and the Future of Social Entrepreneurship." *Journal of Business Ethics* 111, no. 3 (December 2012): 321–334.

Drayton, William. "The Citizen Sector: Becoming as Entrepreneurial and Competitive as Business." *California Management Review* 44, no. 3 (April 2002): 120–132.

Drayton, William. "Everyone a Changemaker: Social Entrepreneurship's Ultimate Goal." *Innovations* 1, no. 1 (Winter 2006): 80–96.

Drayton, William, and Shawn MacDonald. *Leading Public Entrepreneurs*. Arlington, VA: Ashoka, 1993.

Elkington, John, and Pamela Hartigan. *The Power of Unreasonable People: How Social Entrepreneurs Create Markets That Change the World.* Boston: Harvard Business Press, 2008.

Guo, Chao, and Wolfgang Bielefeld. *Social Entrepreneurship: An Evidence-Based Approach to Creating Social Value.* San Francisco: Jossey-Bass, 2014.

Johansson, Frans. *The Medici Effect: What Elephants and Epidemics Can Teach Us About Innovation*. Boston: Harvard Business School Press, 2006.

Kania, John, and Mark Kramer. "Collective Impact." *Stanford Social Innovation Review* 9, no. 1 (Winter 2011): 36–41.

Klein, Maury. *The Change Makers: From Carnegie to Gates, How the Great Entrepreneurs Transformed Ideas into Industries*. New York: Holt, 2004.

Keohane, Georgia Levenson. *Social Entrepreneurship for the 21st Century: Innovation Across the Nonprofit, Private, and Public Sectors*. New York: McGraw-Hill, 2013.

Kristof, Nicholas D., and Sheryl WuDunn. *A Path Appears: Transforming Lives, Creating Opportunity*. New York: Knopf, 2014.

Light, Paul C. "Reshaping Social Entrepreneurship." *Stanford Social Innovation Review* 4, no. 3 (Fall 2006): 47–51.

Light, Paul C. *Driving Social Change: How to Solve the World's Toughest Problems*. Hoboken, NJ: Wiley & Sons, 2010.

Mair, Johanna, Jeffrey Robinson, and Kai Hockerts, eds. *Social Entrepreneurship*. London: Palgrave Macmillan, 2006.

Martin, Roger L. *The Opposable Mind: How Successful Leaders Win Through Integrative Thinking*. Boston: Harvard Business School Press, 2007.

Martin, Roger L., and Sally Osberg. "Social Entrepreneurship: The Case for Definition." *Stanford Social Innovation Review* 5, no. 2 (Spring 2007): 28–39.

McLeod, Heather. "Crossover." *Inc.* May 1997.

Mulgan, Geoff, et al. "Social Innovation: What It Is, Why It Matters and How It Can Be Accelerated." Working paper, Skoll Centre for Social Entrepreneurship, 2007.

Osberg, Sally. "Framing the Change and Changing the Frame: A New Role for Social Entrepreneurs." Opening remarks. *Innovations/Skoll World Forum.* 2009.

Phills, James A. Jr., Kriss Deiglmeier, and Dale T. Miller. "Rediscovering Social Innovation." *Stanford Social Innovation Review* 6, no. 4 (2008): 34–43.

Porter, Michael E., and Mark R. Kramer. "Creating Shared Value." *Harvard Business Review* 89, nos. 1–2 (January–February 2011): 62–77.

Praszkier, Ryszard, and Andrzej Nowak. *Social Entrepreneurship: Theory and Practice.* New York: Cambridge University Press, 2012.

Saul, Jason. *Social Innovation, Inc.: 5 Strategies for Driving Business Growth through Social Change.* San Francisco: Jossey-Bass, 2011.

Schwartz, Beverly. *Rippling: How Social Entrepreneurs Spread Innovation Throughout the World.* San Francisco: Jossey-Bass, 2012.

Seelos, Christian, and Johanna Mair. "Social Entrepreneurship: Creating New Business Models to Serve the Poor" *Business Horizons* 48, no. 3 (2005): 241–246.

Shaprio, Ruth A., ed. *The Real Problem Solvers: Social Entrepreneurs in America.* Stanford, CA: Stanford Business Books, 2013.

Shore, Bill, Darrell Hammond, and Amy Celep. "When Good Is Not Good Enough." *Stanford Social Innovation Review* 11, no. 4 (Fall 2013): 40–47.

Thompson, Laurie Ann. *Be a Changemaker: How to Start Something That Matters.* New York: Simon & Schuster, 2014.

Definitions of Social Entrepreneurship

Bornstein, David, and Susan Davis. *Social Entrepreneurship: What Everyone Needs to Know.* New York: Oxford University Press, 2010.

Bornstein, David. "The Rise of the Social Entrepreneur." *New York Times*, November 13, 2012.

Boschee, Jerr, and Jim McClurg. "Towards a Better Understanding of Social Entrepreneurship: Some Important Distinctions." 2003. http://www.caledonia.org/uk/Papers/social-entrepreneurship.pdf.

Dacin, Peter A., M. Tina Dacin, and Margaret Matear. "Social Entrepreneurship: Why We Don't Need a New Theory and How We Move Forward From Here." *Academy of Management Perspectives* 24, no. 3 (August 2010) 37–57.

Dees, J. Gregory. "The Meaning of 'Social Entrepreneurship.'" Center for Social Innovation, Stanford School of Business, October 31, 1998 (rev.) May 30, 2001. http://csi.gsb.stanford.edu/the-meaning-social-entrepreneurship.

Dees, J. Gregory. "Social Entrepreneurship Is About Innovation and Impact, Not Income." *Social Edge*, September 2003. http://www.caseatduke.org/articles/1004/corner.htm.

Fayolle, Alain, and Harry Matlay, eds. *Handbook of Research on Social Entrepreneurship*. Cheltenham, UK: Edward Elgar Publishing, 2012.

Mair, Johanna, and Ignasi Marti Lanuza. "Social Entrepreneurship Research: A Source of Explanation, Prediction, and Delight." *Journal of World Business* 41, no. 1 (2006): 36–44.

Martin, Roger L., and Sally Osberg. "Social Entrepreneurship: The Case for Definition." *Stanford Social Innovation Review* 5, no. 2 (Spring 2007): 28–39.

Mort, Gillian Sullivan, Jay Weerawardena, and Kashonia Carnegie. "Social Entrepreneurship: Towards Conceptualisation." *International Journal of Nonprofit and Voluntary Sector Marketing* 8, no. 1 (2003): 76–88.

Nicholls, Alex. "The Legitimacy of Social Entrepreneurship: Reflexive Isomorphism in a Pre-Paradigmatic Field." *Entrepreneurship Theory and Practice* 34, no. 4 (July 2010): 611–633.

Nicholls, Alex, ed. *Social Entrepreneurship: New Models of Sustainable Social Change*. New York: Oxford University Press, 2006.

Peredo, Ana Maria, and Murdith McLean. "Social Entrepreneurship: A Critical Review of the Concept." *Journal of World Business* 41, no. 1 (2006): 55–65.

Santos, Filipe M. "A Positive Theory of Social Entrepreneurship." *Journal of Business Ethics* 111, no. 3 (2012): 335–351.

Thompson, John L. "The World of the Social Entrepreneur." *International Journal of Public Sector Management* 15, no. 5 (2002): 412–431.

Thompson, John, Geoff Alvy, and Ann Lees. "Social Entrepreneurship—A New Look at the People and the Potential." *Management Decision* 38, no. 5 (2000): 328–338.

Case Studies

Alvord, Sarah H., L. David Brown, and Christine W. Letts. "Social Entrepreneurship and Social Transformation: An Exploratory Study." Working Paper No. 15. Hauser Center for Nonprofit Organizations, Harvard Kennedy School, Cambridge, MA, November 2002.

Bell, John. *YouthBuild's North Star: A Vision of Greater Potential.* Somerville, MA: YouthBuild USA, 2014.

Bornstein, David. *How to Change the World.* New York: Oxford University Press, 2004.

Bornstein, David. *The Price of a Dream: The Story of Grameen Bank.* New York: Oxford University Press, 1997.

Bornstein, David. "The Rise of the Social Entrepreneur." *New York Times*, November 13, 2012.

Bornstein, David, and Susan Davis. *Social Entrepreneurship: What Everyone Needs to Know.* New York: Oxford University Press, 2010.

Boschee, Jerr. *The Social Enterprise Sourcebook.* Encore! Press, 2001.

Chertavian, Gerald. *A Year Up: How a Pioneering Program Teaches Young Adults Real Skills for Real Jobs—with Real Success.* London: Penguin Books, 2012.

Crutchfield, Leslie R., and Heather McLeod Grant. *Forces for Good: The Six Practices of High-Impact Nonprofits*. San Francisco: Jossey-Bass, 2007.

Elkington, John, and Pamela Hartigan. *The Power of Unreasonable People: How Social Entrepreneurs Create Markets That Change the World.* Boston: Harvard Business Press, 2008.

Farmer, Paul. *Partner to the Poor: A Paul Farmer Reader.* Haun Saussy, ed. Berkeley and Los Angeles, CA: University of California Press, 2010.

Farmer, Paul, and Gustavo Gutiérrez. *In the Company of the Poor: Conversations with Dr. Paul Farmer and Fr. Gustavo Gutiérrez.* Michael Griffin and Jennie Weiss Block, eds. New York: Orbis Books, 2013.

Guclu, Ayse, J. Gregory Dees, and Beth Battle Anderson. "The Growth of YouthBuild: A Case Study." Case SE-02. Duke University Fuqua School of Business, 2004.

Karliner, Josh, Gary Cohen, and Peter Orris. "Lessons in Forging Global Change." *Stanford Social Innovation Review* 12, no. 1 (Winter 2014): 34–39.

Klein, Maury. *The Change Makers: From Carnegie to Gates, How the Great Entrepreneurs Transformed Ideas into Industries*. New York: Holt, 2004.

Kristof, Nicholas D., and Sheryl WuDunn. *Half the Sky: Turning Oppression into Opportunity for Women Worldwide*. New York: Knopf, 2009.

Kristof, Nicholas D., and Sheryl WuDunn. *A Path Appears: Transforming Lives, Creating Opportunity*. New York: Knopf, 2014.

Nicholls, Alex, ed. *Social Entrepreneurship: New Models of Sustainable Social Change*. New York: Oxford University Press, 2006.

Schultz, Ron, ed. *Creating Good Work: The World's Leading Social Entrepreneurs Show How to Build a Healthy Economy.* New York: Palgrave MacMillan, 2013.

Thompson, John L. "The World of the Social Entrepreneur." *International Journal of Public Sector Management* 15, no. 5 (2002): 412–431.

Thurow, Roger. *The Last Hunger Season: A Year in an African Farm Community on the Brink of Change*. New York: PublicAffairs, 2013.

Welch, Wilford. *Tactics of Hope: How Social Entrepreneurs Are Changing Our World*. San Rafael: Earth Aware, 2008.

Autobiographies, Biographies, and Personal Narratives

Bowen, Jenny. *Wish You Happy Forever: What China's Orphans Taught Me About Moving Mountains*. New York: HarperOne, 2014.

Canada, Geoffrey. *Fist, Stick, Knife, Gun: A Personal History of Violence*. Boston: Beacon Press, 2010.

Farmer, Paul. *Haiti After the Earthquake*. New York: PublicAffairs, 2011.

Farmer, Paul. *To Repair the World: Paul Farmer Speaks to the Next Generation*. Jonathan Weigel, ed. Berkeley and Los Angeles, CA: University of California Press, 2013.

Freedman, Marc. *The Big Shift: Navigating the New Stage Beyond Midlife*. New York: PublicAffairs, 2011.

Freedman, Marc. *Encore: Finding Work That Matters in the Second Half of Life*. New York: PublicAffairs, 2007.

Khan, Salman. *The One World Schoolhouse: Education Reimagined*. New York: Hachette Book Group, 2012.

Kidder, Tracy. *Mountains Beyond Mountains: The Quest of Dr. Paul Farmer, A Man Who Would Cure the World*. New York: Random House, 2003.

Kielburger, Craig, and Kevin Major. *Free the Children: A Young Man Fights Against Child Labor and Proves That Children Can Change the World*. New York: HarperCollins, 1998.

Kopp, Wendy. *A Chance to Make History: What Works and What Doesn't in Providing an Excellent Education for All*. New York: PublicAffairs, 2011.

Kopp, Wendy. *One Day All Children . . . The Unlikely Triumph of Teach for America and What I Learned Along the Way*. New York: PublicAffairs, 2001.

Molloy, Aimee. *However Long the Night: Molly Melching's Journey to Help Millions of African Women and Girls Triumph.* New York: HarperCollins, 2013.

Mycoskie, Blake. *Start Something That Matters.* New York: Spiegel & Grau, 2012.

Novogratz, Jacqueline. *The Blue Sweater: Bridging the Gap between Rich and Poor in an Interconnected World.* New York: Rodale, 2009.

Strickland, Bill, and Vince Rause. *Make the Impossible Possible: One Man's Crusade to Inspire Others to Dream Bigger and Achieve the Extraordinary.* New York: Doubleday Broadway Publishing Group, 2007.

Wood, John. *Leaving Microsoft to Change the World: An Entrepreneur's Odyssey to Educate the World's Children.* New York: HarperCollins, 2006.

Social Enterprises, Hybrid Models, and Earned Revenue Streams

Anderson, Steven G. *New Strategies for Social Innovation: Market-Based Approaches for Assisting the Poor.* New York: Columbia University Press, 2014.

Battilana, Julie, Matthew Lee, John Walker, and Cheryl Dorsey. "In Search of the Hybrid Ideal." *Stanford Social Innovation Review* 10, no. 3 (Summer 2012): 51–55.

Boschee, Jerr. *The Social Enterprise Sourcebook.* Encore! Press, 2001.

Brooks, Arthur C. *Social Entrepreneurship: A Modern Approach to Social Value Creation.* Upper Saddle River, NJ: Pearson Prentice Hall, 2008.

Clark, Catherine H., and Selen Uçak. "RISE For-Profit Social Entrepreneur Report: Balancing Markets and Values." Research Initiative on Social Entrepreneurship, 2006. http://www.riseproject.org/rise-sep-report.pdf.

Dart, Raymond. "The Legitimacy of Social Enterprise." *Nonprofit Management and Leadership* 14, no. 4 (Summer 2004): 411–424.

Dees, J. Gregory. "Enterprising Nonprofits." *Harvard Business Review* 76, no. 1 (January 1998): 54–67.

Eikenberry, Angela M., and Jodie Drapal Kluver. "The Marketization of the Nonprofit Sector: Civil Society at Risk?" *Public Administration Review* 64, no. 2 (March 2004): 132–140.

Elkington, John. *Cannibals with Forks: The Triple Bottom Line of 21st Century Business*. Oxford: Capstone/John Wiley, 1997.

Emerson, Jed, and Fay Twersky, eds. *New Social Entrepreneurs: The Success, Challenge and Lessons of Non-Profit Enterprise Creation*. Roberts Foundation: 1996.

Firstenberg, Paul B. *Managing for Profit in the Nonprofit World*. Foundation Center, 1986.

Foster, William, and Jeffrey L. Bradach. "Should Nonprofits Seek Profits?" *Harvard Business Review* 83, no. 2 (February 2005): 92–100.

Institute for Social Entrepreneurs. "Evolution of the Social Enterprise Industry: A Chronology of Key Events." August 2008. https://www.se-alliance.org/upload/Membership%20Pages/evolution.pdf.

MacMillan, Ian C., and James D. Thompson. *The Social Entrepreneur's Playbook: Pressure Test, Plan, Launch and Scale Your Enterprise*. Philadelphia: Wharton Digital Press, 2013.

Prahalad, C. K. *The Fortune at the Bottom of the Pyramid: Eradicating Poverty through Profits*. Philadelphia: Wharton School Publishing, 2006.

Skloot, Edward. *The Nonprofit Entrepreneur: Creating Ventures to Earn Income*. Foundation Center: 1988.

Skloot, Edward. "Should Not-for-Profits Go into Business?" *Harvard Business Review* 61, no. 1 (January–February 1983): 20–26.

Wei-Skillern, Jane, James E. Austin, Herman B. Leonard, and Howard H. Stevenson. *Entrepreneurship in the Social Sector*. London: Sage, 2007.

Yunus, Muhammad. *Banker to the Poor: Micro-Lending and the Battle Against World Poverty*. New York: PublicAffairs, 1999.

Yunus, Muhammad. *Creating a World without Poverty: Social Business and the Future of Capitalism*. New York: PublicAffairs, 2007.

Yunus, Muhammad. "Social Business Entrepreneurs Are the Solution." Paper presented at the Skoll World Forum on Social Entrepreneurship, Oxford, March 2006.

Yunus, Muhammad, Frédéric Dalsace, David Menascé, and Bénédicte Faivre-Tavignot. "Reaching the Rich World's Poorest Consumers." *Harvard Business Review* 92, no. 3 (March 2015): 46–53.

Scaling Impact, Collective Impact, and Social Innovation

Bloom, Paul N., and J. Gregory Dees. "Cultivate Your Ecosystem." *Stanford Social Innovation Review* 6, no. 1 (2008): 47–53.

Bloom, Paul N., and Edward Skloot, eds. *Scaling Social Impact: New Thinking*. New York: Palgrave MacMillan, 2010.

Bradach, Jeffrey. "Scaling Impact." *Stanford Social Innovation Review* 8, no. 3 (Summer 2010): 27–28.

Bradach, Jeffrey, and Abe Grindle. "Transformative Scale: The Future of Growing What Works." *Stanford Social Innovation Review*, February 19, 2014. www.ssireview.org/articles/entry/transformative_scale_the_future_of_growing_what_works.

Christensen, Clayton M., Heiner Baumann, Rudy Ruggles, and Thomas M. Sadtler. "Disruptive Innovation for Social Change." *Harvard Business Review* 84, no. 12 (December 2006): 94–101.

Dees, J. Gregory, and Beth Battle Anderson. "Scaling Social Impact." *Stanford Social Innovation Review* 1, no. 4 (Spring 2004).

Drayton, Bill. "Tipping the World: The Power of Collaborative Entrepreneurship." *Voices on Society: What Matters*. McKinsey & Company, April 2010.

Goldsmith, Stephen, et al. *The Power of Social Innovation: How Civic Entrepreneurs Ignite Community Networks for Good.* San Francisco: Jossey-Bass, 2010.

Hanleybrown, Fay, John Kania, and Mark Kramer. "Channeling Change: Making Collective Impact Work." *Stanford Social Innovation Review*, January 26, 2012. http://www.ssireview.org/blog/entry/channeling_change_making_collective_impact_work.

Light, Paul C. *Driving Social Change: How to Solve the World's Toughest Problems*. Hoboken, NJ: Wiley & Sons, 2011.

Mulgan, Geoff. "The Process of Social Innovation." *Innovations* 1, no. 2 (Spring 2006): 145–162.

Murray, Robin, Julie Caulier-Grice, and Geoff Mulgan. "The Open Book of Social Innovation." March 2010. http://youngfoundation.org/publications/the-open-book-of-social-innovation.

Seelos, Christian, and Johanna Mair. "Innovation Is Not the Holy Grail." *Stanford Social Innovation Review* 10, no. 4 (Fall 2012): 44–49.

Senge, Peter, Hal Hamilton, and John Kania. "The Dawn of System Leadership." *Stanford Social Innovation Review* 13, no. 1 (Winter 2015): 26–33.

Not-for-Profit Management: Best Practices and How-To Guides

Boschee, Jerr. *Merging Mission and Money: A Board Member's Guide to Social Entrepreneurship*. National Center for Nonprofit Boards, 1998.

Boschee, Jerr. *Migrating from Innovation to Entrepreneurship: How Nonprofits Are Moving toward Sustainability and Self-Sufficiency*. Encore! Press, 2006.

Boschee, Jerr. *The Social Enterprise Sourcebook*. Encore! Press, 2001.

Brooks, Arthur C. *Social Entrepreneurship: A Modern Approach to Social Value Creation*. Upper Saddle River, NJ: Pearson Prentice Hall, 2008.

Collins, Jim. *Good to Great and the Social Sectors: A Monograph to Accompany Good to Great*. New York: HarperCollins, 2005.

Crutchfield, Leslie R., and Heather McLeod Grant. *Forces for Good: The Six Practices of High-Impact Nonprofits*. San Francisco: Jossey-Bass, 2008.

Dees, J. Gregory. "Enterprising Nonprofits: What Do You Do When Traditional Sources of Funding Fall Short?" *Harvard Business Review* 77, no. 1 (January 1998): 54–67.

Dees, J. Gregory, Jed Emerson, and Peter Economy. *Enterprising Nonprofits: A Toolkit for Social Entrepreneurs*. New York: John Wiley and Sons, 2001.

Emerson, Jed, and Fay Twersky, eds. *New Social Entrepreneurs: The Success, Challenge and Lessons of Non-Profit Enterprise Creation*. Roberts Foundation: 1996.

Firstenberg, Paul B. *Managing for Profit in the Nonprofit World*. Foundation Center: 1986.

Foster, William, and Jeffrey L. Bradach. "Should Nonprofits Seek Profits?" *Harvard Business Review* 83, no. 2 (February 2005): 92–100.

Guo, Chao, and Wolfgang Bielefeld. *Social Entrepreneurship: An Evidence-Based Approach to Creating Social Value*. San Francisco: Jossey-Bass, 2014.

MacMillan, Ian C., and James D. Thompson. *The Social Entrepreneur's Playbook, Expanded Edition: Pressure Test, Plan, Launch and Scale Your Social Enterprise*. Philadelphia: Wharton Digital Press, 2013.

Scofield, Rupert. *The Social Entrepreneur's Handbook: How to Start, Build, and Run a Business That Improves the World*. New York: McGraw-Hill, 2011.

Skloot, Edward. *The Nonprofit Entrepreneur: Creating Ventures to Earn Income*. Foundation Center, 1988.

Skloot, Edward. "Should Not-for-Profits Go into Business?" *Harvard Business Review* 61, no. 1 (January–February 1983): 20–26.

Wolk, Andrew, and Kelley Kreitz. *Business Planning for Enduring Social Impact*. Cambridge, MA: Root Cause Publishing, 2008.

Academic Perspectives on Social Entrepreneurship

Alvord, Sarah H., L. David Brown, and Christine W. Letts. "Social Entrepreneurship and Social Transformation: An Exploratory Study." Working Paper No. 15. Hauser Center for Nonprofit

Organizations, Harvard Kennedy School, Cambridge, MA, November 2002.

Anderson, Steven G. *New Strategies for Social Innovation: Market-Based Approaches for Assisting the Poor.* New York: Columbia University Press, 2014.

Austin, James, Howard Stevenson, and Jane Wei-Skillern. "Social and Commercial Entrepreneurship: Same, Different, or Both?" *Entrepreneurship Theory and Practice* 30, no. 1 (January 2006): 1–22.

Borzaga, Carlo, and Jacques Defourny, eds. *The Emergence of Social Enterprise.* Routledge Studies in the Management of Voluntary and Non-Profit Organizations. London and New York: Routledge, 2001.

Dacin, M. Tina, Peter A. Dacin, and Paul Tracey. "Social Entrepreneurship: A Critique and Future Directions." *Organization Science* 22, no. 5 (March 2011): 1203–1213.

Dacin, Peter A., M. Tina Dacin, and Margaret Matear. "Social Entrepreneurship: Why We Don't Need a New Theory and How We Move Forward From Here." *Academy of Management Perspectives* 24, no. 3 (August 2010): 37–57.

Dart, Raymond. "The Legitimacy of Social Enterprise." *Nonprofit Management and Leadership* 14, no. 4 (2004): 411–424.

Defourny, Jacques, and Marthe Nyssens. "Conceptions of Social Enterprise and Social Entrepreneurship in Europe and the United States: Convergences and Divergences." *Journal of Social Entrepreneurship* 1, no. 1 (2010): 32–53.

Eikenberry, Angela M., and Jodie Drapal Kluver. "The Marketization of the Nonprofit Sector: Civil Society at Risk?" *Public Administration Review* 64, no. 2 (March 2004): 132–140.

Fayolle, Alain, and Harry Matlay, eds. *Handbook of Research on Social Entrepreneurship.* Cheltenham, UK: Edward Elgar Publishing, 2012.

Mair, Johanna, and Ignasi Marti Lanuza. "Social Entrepreneurship Research: A Source of Explanation, Prediction, and Delight." *Journal of World Business* 41, no. 1 (2006): 36–44.

Mair, Johanna, Jeffrey Robinson, and Kai Hockerts, eds. *Social Entrepreneurship*. London: Palgrave Macmillan, 2006.

Mort, Gillian Sullivan, Jay Weerawardena, and Kashonia Carnegie. "Social Entrepreneurship: Towards Conceptualisation." *International Journal of Nonprofit and Voluntary Sector Marketing* 8, no. 1 (2003): 76–88.

Mosher-Williams, Rachel, ed. *Research on Social Entrepreneurship: Understanding and Contributing to an Emerging Field*. Washington, DC: Aspen Institute, 2006.

Nicholls, Alex. "The Legitimacy of Social Entrepreneurship: Reflexive Isomorphism in a Pre-Paradigmatic Field." *Entrepreneurship Theory and Practice* 34, no. 4 (July 2010): 611–633.

Nicholls, Alex, ed. *Social Entrepreneurship: New Models of Sustainable Social Change*. New York: Oxford University Press, 2006.

Peredo, Ana Maria, and Murdith McLean. "Social Entrepreneurship: A Critical Review of the Concept." *Journal of World Business* 41, no. 1 (2006), 55–65.

Santos, Filipe. "A Positive Theory of Social Entrepreneurship." *Journal of Business Ethics* 111, no. 3 (2012): 335–351.

Shaw, Eleanor, and Sara Carter. "Social Entrepreneurship: Theoretical Antecedents and Empirical Analysis of Entrepreneurial Processes and Outcomes." *Journal of Small Business and Enterprise Development* 14, no. 3 (2007): 418–434.

Short, Jeremy C., Todd W. Moss, and G. T. Lumpkin. "Research in Social Entrepreneurship: Past Contributions and Future Opportunities." *Strategic Entrepreneurship Journal* 3, no. 2 (2009): 161–194.

Thompson, John, Geoff Alvy, and Ann Lees. "Social Entrepreneurship—A New Look at the People and the Potential." *Management Decision* 38, no. 5 (2000): 328–338.

Weerawardena, Jay, and Gillian Sullivan Mort. "Investigating Social Entrepreneurship: A Multidimensional Model." *Journal of World Business* 41, no. 1 (2006): 21–35.

History and Evolution of Social Entrepreneurship

Anderson, Steven G. *New Strategies for Social Innovation: Market-Based Approaches for Assisting the Poor.* New York: Columbia University Press, 2014.

Borzaga, Carlo, and Jacques Defourny, eds. *The Emergence of Social Enterprise.* Routledge Studies in the Management of Voluntary and Non-Profit Organizations. London and New York: Routledge, 2001.

Dart, Raymond. "The Legitimacy of Social Enterprise." *Nonprofit Management and Leadership* 14, no. 4 (Summer 2004): 411–424.

Dees, J. Gregory. "The Meaning of Social Entrepreneurship." Center for Social Innovation, Stanford School of Business, October 31, 1998; (rev.) May 30, 2001. http://csi.gsb.stanford.edu/the-meaning-social-entrepreneurship.

Defourny, Jacques, and Marthe Nyssens. "Conceptions of Social Enterprise and Social Entrepreneurship in Europe and the United States: Convergences and Divergences." *Journal of Social Entrepreneurship* 1, no. 1 (2010): 32–53.

Institute for Social Entrepreneurs. "Evolution of the Social Enterprise Industry: A Chronology of Key Events." August 2008. https://www.se-alliance.org/upload/Membership%20Pages/evolution.pdf.

Leadbeater, Charles. *The Rise of the Social Entrepreneur.* Demos, 1997.

Mosher-Williams, Rachel, ed. *Research on Social Entrepreneurship: Understanding and Contributing to an Emerging Field.* Washington, DC: Aspen Institute, 2006.

Nicholls, Alex, ed. *Social Entrepreneurship: New Models of Sustainable Social Change.* New York: Oxford University Press, 2006.

Shaw, Eleanor, and Sara Carter. "Social Entrepreneurship: Theoretical Antecedents and Empirical Analysis of Entrepreneurial Processes and Outcomes." *Journal of Small Business and Enterprise Development* 14, no. 3 (2007): 418–434.

Philanthropy and Impact Investing

Arrillaga-Andreessen, Laura. *Giving 2.0: Transform Your Giving and Our World*. San Francisco: Jossey-Bass, 2012.

Bishop, Matthew, and Michael Green. *Philanthrocapitalism: How the Rich Can Save the World*. New York: Bloomsbury Press, 2008.

Brest, Paul, and Hal Harvey. *Money Well Spent: A Strategic Plan for Smart Philanthropy*. New York: Bloomberg Press, 2008.

Bugg-Levine, Antony, and Jed Emerson. *Impact Investing: Transforming How We Make Money While Making a Difference*. San Francisco: Jossey-Bass, 2011.

Clark, Cathy, Jed Emerson, and Ben Thornley. *The Impact Investor: Lessons in Leadership and Strategy for Collaborative Capitalism*. San Francisco: Jossey-Bass, 2015.

Dichter, Sasha, Robert Katz, Harvey Koh, and Ashish Karamchandani. "Closing the Pioneer Gap." *Stanford Social Innovation Review* 11, no. 1 (Winter 2013): 36–43.

Keohane, Georgia Levenson. "The Rise and (Potential) Fall of Philanthrocapitalism." *Slate*, November 13, 2008. http://www.slate.com/articles/life/philanthropy/2008/11/the_rise_and_potential_fall_of_philanthrocapitalism.html.

Letts, Christine W., William P. Ryan, and Allen S. Grossman. "Virtuous Capital: What Foundations Can Learn from Venture Capitalists." *Harvard Business Review* 76, no. 3 (April 1997).

Monitor Institute. *Investing for Social and Environmental Impact*. Boston: Monitor, 2009.

Corporate Responsibility and Entrepreneurship

Anderson, Steven G. *New Strategies for Social Innovation: Market-Based Approaches for Assisting the Poor*. New York: Columbia University Press, 2014.

Austin, James, Howard Stevenson, and Jane Wei-Skillern. "Social and Commercial Entrepreneurship: Same, Different, or Both?" *Entrepreneurship Theory and Practice* 30, no. 1 (January 2006): 1–22.

Deakins, David, and Mark Freel. *Entrepreneurship and Small Firms.* London: McGraw-Hill, 2006.

Drucker, Peter F. *Innovation and Entrepreneurship.* New York: HarperCollins, 1985.

Elkington, John. *Cannibals with Forks: The Triple Bottom Line of 21st Century Business.* Oxford: Capstone/John Wiley, 1997.

Elkington, John. *The Chrysalis Economy: How Citizen CEOs and Corporations Can Fuse Values and Value Creation.* Oxford: Capstone/John Wiley, 2001.

Gergen, Christopher, and Gregg Vanourek. *Life Entrepreneurs: Ordinary People Creating Extraordinary Lives.* San Francisco: Jossey-Bass, 2008.

Johnson, Steven. *Where Good Ideas Come From: The Natural History of Innovation.* New York: Penguin Group, 2011.

Leadbeater, Charles. *The Frugal Innovator: Creating Change on a Shoestring Budget.* London: Palgrave Macmillan, 2014.

Martin, Roger L. *The Opposable Mind: How Successful Leaders Win Through Integrative Thinking.* Boston: Harvard Business School Press, 2007.

Martin, Roger L. "The Virtue Matrix: Calculating the Return on Corporate Social Responsibility." *Harvard Business Review* 80, no. 3 (March 2002): 68–75.

Rindova, Violina, Daved Barry, and David J. Ketchen, Jr. "Entrepreneuring as Emancipation." *Academy of Management Review* 34, no. 3 (2009): 477–491.

Rottenberg, Linda. *Crazy Is a Compliment: The Power of Zigging When Everyone Else Zags.* New York: Penguin, 2014.

Steyaert, Chris, and Daniel Hjorth, eds. *Entrepreneurship as Social Change: A Third Movements in Entrepreneurship Book.* Cheltenham, UK: Edward Elgar Publishing, 2008.

Index

Acknowledgments

Our decision to hunker down to think, research, and ultimately write *Getting Beyond Better: How Social Entrepreneurship Works* came about for one reason, and one reason only—a desire to share what we've learned in order to help unleash the promise of this still-nascent field. From our unique vantage point at the Skoll Foundation, we've had the privilege of getting to know hundreds of women and men on the front lines of social change. Over the past decade-plus, they've shown us what it takes and what they need to achieve their ambitions for change. We are grateful to have the chance to thank them, along with the many other wonderful people who have made this book possible.

First and foremost is Jeff Skoll, Chairman and founder of the Skoll Foundation. Jeff is himself the quintessential social entrepreneur. As such, he was quick to spot and characterize a "special kind of leader," the social entrepreneur, who brought the creativity, discipline, and drive of a business entrepreneur to the challenge of solving global problems. Jeff then took a museum CEO (Sally) and a business school dean (Roger) and thrust us into an exciting field at a seminal time, providing unflagging leadership, inspiration, and support to our efforts over the years. This book would have had no chance of happening had it not been for Jeff. We are also deeply appreciative of the Foundation's board directors, all of whom have contributed generously of their time and wisdom to building the Skoll portfolio. They include Jim DeMartini, Debra Dunn, Peter Hero, Larry Brilliant, and Kirk Hanson.

Jennifer Riel, at the Rotman School of Management, has been our editor extraordinaire. She orchestrated the creation of this book with expertise, style, and good humor. As we tested examples, drew them out, added new ones, and changed the flow of the through-line, she kept the reader's interest front and center: a compelling narrative for this important material. Thank you, Jennifer, for making the book so much better than it would have been without your professional dedication. Also at the Rotman School, Quinn Davidson was a great support throughout the project, Darren Karn provided research support, and Nogah Kornberg was an early, thoughtful reader of the manuscript.

Cindy Chen, of the Skoll Foundation, has been our invaluable organizer. A complex research and writing venture like this one needs someone with a first-rate and disciplined mind to keep every piece on the straight and narrow, from the theory development on one end of the spectrum to the editing schedule on the other—and literally everything in between. Thank you, Cindy, for helping us get to the finish line. Many other colleagues at the Skoll Foundation also had a hand in evolving the theory and compiling information. Richard Fahey, Renee Kaplan, Judy Parkman, Ed Diener, Sandy Herz, Suzana Grego, Edwin Ou, Ehren Reed, Laura Vais, Sarah Borgman, Paula Kravitz, and Talia Means have been wonderful partners over the years this book has been in the making.

In addition, we have benefited from many exceptional allies and partners. We are humbled to acknowledge how much we've learned from Muhammad Yunus, Sir Ronald

Cohen, Nandan Nilekani, Bill Drayton, David Bornstein, Stephan Chambers, Pamela Hartigan, Alex Nicholls, Jacqueline Novogratz, Cathy Clark, and others who have invested so much in strengthening the field and practice of social entrepreneurship.

We are also extremely grateful to our friend Arianna Huffington, an awesome change agent in her own right, for taking the time out of her demanding schedule to write the foreword for this book. Arianna is a tremendous champion for social entrepreneurs (many of whom blog on her platform), and it is an honor to include her insights in the book. As Arianna redefines a "third metric" of success for her legions of admirers, she can count on support from the burgeoning community of fellow-traveler social entrepreneurs!

As authors and editors get deeper into their work, myopia can set in; this is where outside readers can make a huge difference. They help us understand what makes sense or doesn't and where we need to expand or cut back. We were fortunate that some smart and accomplished folks, including Michael Green, Ruth Norris, and Justin Ferrell, took the time to read the manuscript and make smart and helpful comments. Thanks to each of you for making this a better book.

Our friends at Harvard Business Review Press have been superb partners over the course of this journey. Jeff Kehoe acquired the book and has been a faithful supporter and astute commentator throughout our research and writing process. His own dedication of time and intellect to engage substantively with social entrepreneurship, together with his prodding and encouragement, has impressed us: the book is stronger by far for his commitment.

Ultimately, this book exists thanks to the visions and impact of those comprising our cadre of Skoll Awards for Social Entrepreneurship winners. We studied them, interviewed them, chronicled them, and challenged them to go deeper in revealing the thinking and experiences that informed their actions. Their stories, setbacks, revelations, and achievements make the book. As with every publication, we acknowledge with more than a twinge of sadness how much great material ended up on the cutting room floor. We truly wish there had been room for every story of change-in-progress! So it is with full hearts that we thank all of the 91 organizations and 112 individual social entrepreneurs comprising the Skoll community. We are proud to invite readers to learn more about them by accessing their profiles on the Skoll Foundation website, www.skollfoundation.org.

While our research process was comprehensive in considering all the social entrepreneurs represented in the Skoll portfolio, we asked a lot from several of them. Special thanks for going the distance with us to Mark Plotkin and Liliana Madrigal (Amazon Conservation Team), Bart Weetjens (APOPO), Ann Cotton (Campaign for Female Education), Mindy Lubber (Ceres), Taddy Blecher (Community and Individual Development Association), Vicky Colbert (Escuela Nueva Foundation), Paul Rice (Fair Trade USA), Luis Oquiñena (Gawad Kalinga), Nina Smith and Kailash Satyarthi (GoodWeave), Joe Madiath (Gram Vikas), Adalberto Veríssimo and Carlos Souza Jr. (Imazon), Carne Ross (Independent Diplomat), Matt Flannery and Premal Shah (Kiva), Tim Hanstad (Landesa), Rupert Howes (Marine Stewardship Council), Ellen Moir (New Teacher Center), Andrew Youn (One Acre Fund), Dr. Paul Farmer

(Partners in Health), Madhav Chavan (Pratham), Debbie Aung Din and Jim Taylor (Proximity Designs), Andrea Coleman and Barry Coleman (Riders for Health), William Foote (Root Capital), Molly Melching (Tostan), Cecilia Flores-Oebanda (Visayan Forum Foundation), and Gary White (Water.org).

Finally, we hope that this book will make a contribution to the development of what we believe is a domain of exceptional promise. Populated by some of the smartest, hardest-working, and most dedicated people on the planet, the field of social entrepreneurship needs all of us to achieve its potential. We invite you to learn more, and to join us!

About the Authors

Roger L. Martin is an acclaimed author, consultant, and professor. He is Director of the Martin Prosperity Institute at the Rotman School of Management, University of Toronto. He served as Dean of the Rotman School from 1998 to 2013. Prior to Rotman, he spent thirteen years as a Director of Monitor Company, a global strategy consulting firm, where he served as cohead of the firm for two years. He has been a board member of the Skoll Foundation since its inception.

Roger is an adviser to CEOs on strategy, design, innovation, and integrative thinking. He has written widely on these subjects and has published eight books, including *Playing to Win* (with A.G. Lafley), *Fixing the Game*, *The Design of Business*, and *The Opposable Mind.*

In 2013 Roger placed third on the Thinkers50 list, a biennial ranking of the most influential business thinkers in the world. In 2010 he was named one of the twenty-seven most influential designers in the world by *Bloomberg Business.*

A Canadian from Wallenstein, Ontario, Roger received his AB degree in economics from Harvard College in 1979 and his MBA from Harvard Business School in 1981.

Sally R. Osberg is President and CEO of the Skoll Foundation, which supports social entrepreneurs whose proven models are driving solutions to many of the world's most pressing problems. She is a founding director of the Social Progress Imperative and serves on the Advisory

Council of The Elders—an independent group of global leaders who work together for peace and human rights—and on the boards of the Oracle Education Foundation, the Skoll Global Threats Fund, and the Palestine-based Partners for Sustainable Development.

Sally's articles on philanthropy and social entrepreneurship have appeared online and in leading sector publications. She has also contributed interviews and chapters to *Social Entrepreneurship: New Models of Sustainable Social Change, Philanthropy in the 21st Century,* and *The Real Problem Solvers.*

Prior to the Skoll Foundation, Sally was founding Executive Director of the Children's Discovery Museum of San Jose.

She has been recognized as one of Silicon Valley's Millennium 100 by the *San Jose Mercury News* and among the social sector's 50 most influential leaders by *The NonProfit Times.*

Raised in New York, Sally has spent most of her adult life in California. She graduated with a BA in literature from Scripps College and received her MA from Claremont Graduate University.